Leeds Trinity
All Saints

SOCIAL CHANGE AND CONTINUITY

T.

D1100286

207887 5

Social Change and Continuity: England 1550–1750

Revised Edition

BARRY COWARD

LONGMAN

LONDON AND NEW YORK

941·06 coco

Addison Wesley Longman Limited
Edinburgh Gate,
Harlow, Essex CM20 2JE,
United Kingdom
and Associated Companies throughout the world.

Published in the United States of America
by Addison Wesley Longman Inc., New York

© Addison Wesley Longman Limited 1988, 1997

The right of Barry Coward to be identified
as author of this Work has been asserted by him
in accordance with the Copyright, Designs and
Patents Act 1988.

All rights reserved; no part of the publication may be
reproduced, stored in a retrieval system, or transmitted
in any form or by an means, electronic, mechanical,
photocopying, recording, or otherwise, without either the
prior written permission of the Publishers or a licence
permitting restricted copying issued by the
Copyright Licensing Agency Ltd.,
90 Tottenham Court Road, London W1P 9HE.

First published 1988
Fourth impression 1995
Revised Edition 1997

ISBN 0 582 294428 PPR

British Library Cataloguing in Publication Data

A catalogue record for this book is available from the British Library

Library of Congress Cataloging-in-Publication Data

Coward, Barry.
  [Social change and continuity in early modern England, 1550–1750]
  Social change and continuity: England 1550–1750 / Barry Coward.-- Rev. ed.
      p. cm. -- (Seminar studies in history)
  Rev. ed. of: Social change and continuity in early modern England, 1550–1750. 1988.
  Includes bibliographical references and index.
  ISBN 0-582-29442-8
    1. England--Social conditions--16th century. 2. England--Social
  conditions--17th century. 3. England--Social conditions--18th century. I. Coward,
  Barry. Social change and continuity in early modern England, 1550–1750. II. Title.
  III. Series.
  HN398.E5C68 1997
  306'.0942--dc21   97-4237
                                                                    CIP

Set by 7 in 10/12 Sabon
Transferred to digital print on demand 2003
Printed & Bound by Antony Rowe Ltd, Eastbourne

CONTENTS

AN INTRODUCTION TO THE SERIES

Such is the pace of historical enquiry in the modern world that there is an ever-widening gap between the specialist article or monograph, incorporating the results of current research, and general surveys, which inevitably become out of date. *Seminar Studies in History* are designed to bridge this gap. The series was founded by Patrick Richardson in 1966 and his aim was to cover major themes in British, European and World history. Between 1980 and 1996 Roger Lockyer continued his work, before handing the editorship over to Clive Emsley and Gordon Martel. Clive Emsley is Professor of History at the Open University, while Gordon Martel is Professor of International History at the University of Northern British Columbia, Canada and Senior Research Fellow at De Montfort University.

All the books are written by experts in their field who are not only familiar with the latest research but have often contributed to it. They are frequently revised, in order to take account of new information and interpretations. They provide a selection of documents to illustrate major themes and provoke discussion, and also a guide to further reading. The aim of *Seminar Studies* is to clarify complex issues without over-simplifying them, and to stimulate readers into deepening their knowledge and understanding of major themes and topics.

NOTE ON REFERENCING SYSTEM

Readers should note that numbers in square brackets [5] refer them to the corresponding entry in the Bibliography at the end of the book (specific page numbers are given in italics). A number in square brackets preceded by *Doc.* [*Doc.* 5] refers readers to the corresponding item in the Documents section which follows the main text.

PART ONE: THE STRUCTURE OF EARLY MODERN ENGLISH SOCIETY

1 THE SOCIAL ORDER IN EARLY MODERN ENGLAND

The first major problem facing social historians of early modern England is to find ways to describe its social structure. One possible solution is to apply concepts and terminology used to describe either the industrialised society of nineteenth- and twentieth-century Britain, like 'class', or the societies of traditional, Third World countries, like 'peasantry'. This is tempting, since early modern England was not a 'pre-industrialised' society, and recent writing has weakened the idea that in a few decades after 1780 English society was suddenly and fundamentally transformed by 'The Industrial Revolution' [29]. Furthermore, early modern English society had characteristics in common with some present-day underdeveloped countries: a fragile agrarian economy, widespread underemployment and a massive poverty problem. Yet these similarities ought not to obscure some basic differences between early modern English society and other societies both at the time and later that will become apparent in what follows. A central feature of early modern English society that this book seeks to underline is its *distinctiveness*.

So, how should one describe a society that was different in many respects from both modern industrialised and underdeveloped societies? Contemporary descriptions – what people of early modern England thought their society was like – are the best guides. When using the writings of contemporaries, however, it is essential to make clear a distinction between those who described their society as they wanted it to be and those who described society as they saw it. A recurrent literary theme from the sixteenth to the eighteenth centuries is the superiority of an idealised fixed society in which people remained in the 'degree' into which they had been born, rather than a fluid, changing society. It was essential for good social and political order, it was believed, that the rich should remain rich and the poor remain poor. This state of affairs was held to be ordained by God as an indispensable part of a unified and ordered universe. In the sixteenth century this 'world picture' was most frequently expressed by the idea of the Great Chain of Being, which has received widespread attention from both historians and specialists in the literature of Elizabethan England [23]. Less widely studied, but equally important, is the persistence of this idea in the seventeenth and early eighteenth centuries, when writers like Nathaniel Crouch in 1681 [*Doc. 2*] and Robert Moss in 1708 elaborated on the same theme as that developed by the anonymous author of *The Homily of Obedience* in 1547.

Nor was this ideal expressed only in print. The perceived necessity of an hierarchical, fixed society as a precondition of social stability [*Doc. 1*] accounts for the many elaborate devices used to emphasise the existing social order. Much more so than in modern times extraordinary care was taken to ensure, for example, that where people stood in ceremonial processions, where they sat in church, the order in which they were listed in official documents, and the ways they were addressed all accorded with their perceived ranking in society. Attempts were even made in the sixteenth century to force people to wear the type and quality of cloth and ornaments appropriate to their status in order to make plain the distinctiveness of social 'degrees' [16]. Yet, the frequent emphasis on an ideal 'world picture' and the importance of precedence reflects (and was a reaction to) the fact that in reality early modern English society, though highly stratified, was not rigidly fixed; rather, it was more fluid, open and characterised by more upward and downward mobility than many conservative-minded contemporaries would have liked, for reasons that will be discussed in Chapter 2.

Fortunately, there was a second group of writers in early modern England who attempted to describe society as they saw it and who laid less stress on society as they would have liked it to be [13]. For that reason the writings of sixteenth-century social commentators like Sir Thomas Smith [*Doc. 3*], William Harrison and Thomas Wilson and the more elaborate statistical analyses of William Petty, Gregory King and others published in the seventeenth and eighteenth centuries provide the best starting-point for an understanding of the structure of early modern English society [339; 342; 348; 350; 354].

There are two features of their analyses that are especially valuable. First, they recognised, not always approvingly, that social changes *were* taking place. Sir Thomas Smith's comment that 'gentlemen be made good cheap' [*Doc. 3*] illustrates that even the biggest gulf in early modern English society, that separating gentlemen from the rest, could be bridged [*Doc. 17*]. Secondly, they provide a good basis on which to build an acceptable working description of the social order of early modern England. Their methods of classifying individuals into social groups vary, but most of them recognised that social status was decided by a mixture of determinants: blood ties, marriage, the type of office held or lifestyle adopted and especially by wealth. The resulting social framework (as they saw it) was an hierarchical one with a class of 'gentlemen' at its apex. Gentility had lost its military function by the sixteenth century and what now bound all gentlemen together was not the freedom to bear arms, but the possession of sufficient wealth to enable leisure and free time to be devoted to the service of the commonwealth. There were differences of wealth and status between gentlemen, a fact which contemporaries recognised by detailed discussions of the differences between those who held titles of peerages (dukes, marquises, earls, viscounts, barons and, from 1611, baronets), knights, esquires and mere 'gentlemen'. But contemporary commentators were (rightly) quick to emphasise that these differences were less important than the gulf which separated this premier social group in English landed society from those who were not 'gentlemen'. These were those who did not possess enough wealth to give them leisure and independence, and in the strict hierarchy of landed society the most wealthy of these non-gentlemen were usually called 'yeomen' and the less wealthy 'husbandmen'. The use of these terms by social commentators and also by others in official documents and in letters is too frequent for them to be ignored and suggests that they accorded with social reality. The differences between yeomen and husbandmen were great, although, unlike gentlemen, both had to work with their hands for a living as farmers. Yeomen might be owner-occupiers or tenants of others but the basic determinant of their social status was the amount of land they farmed; yeomen were large farmers. Husbandmen, on the other hand, were much poorer and often farmed little more than smallholdings. Sometimes they are difficult to distinguish from labourers and servants, the social groups at the base of the pyramid of society. As will be seen, recent work has shown that these dependent people were not an undifferentiated social mass, but the contemporary practice of treating them as one broad group does seem to be a useful one.

The more one reads the writings of contemporary commentators, however, the more it becomes clear that their classifications do not provide a *complete* description of the social order. What gaps in their analyses need to be filled? The first and largest is the omission of women. All contemporary social commentators were men and they describe an adult, male society. This is not surprising given the patriarchal nature of early modern society and the subservient position women were expected to have in it. As will be seen, the household was the basic unit of society, and women, like children and servants, were dependants of the male heads of households – their roles and status were not considered worthy of separate treatment. Such an omission obviously vitiates the usefulness of contemporary analyses, leaving a wide gap in the social history of the period that is only slowly being filled.

Most contemporary descriptions are similarly uninformative about regional variations. William Harrison's vital qualification that improved living standards in his own day (the later sixteenth century) were limited to 'these southern parts' [352 *pp*. 69–70] is a rare reference in this type of writing to the enormous regional disparities in the distribution of wealth between the poorer northern and western counties and the more prosperous south and east, which is illustrated in subsidy assessments [20]. Nor do these writings reflect regional variations in economic and social structures that cut across the basic north west/south east division. Again it has been left to social historians to devise ways of describing and analysing regional differences in social structures and the nature of social change.

Perhaps the most important amendment of all that needs to be made to the contemporary descriptions of the social order already mentioned is to clarify the position of those social groups that do not fit easily into an hierarchy of *landed* society. The most important attempt by other contemporaries to deal with this problem is by what K. Wrightson (in [10]) has called 'the language of sorts', used at first in a simple two-part model ('the better sort' and 'the poorer sort'), to which many commentators later added a third group, 'the middling sort'. Faced with the task of describing a period of rapid social change, 'the language of sorts' has as many attractions for social historians of early modern England as it had for contemporaries. Not the least of these is the use of 'the middling sort' as a means of identifying the unprecedented expansion in early modern England of the numbers of merchants, craftsmen and professional people, as well as substantial farmers, that do not fit easily into analytical models based on 'rank' and 'degree'. It has consequently been enthusiastically adopted by historians who see a need to write the social history of early modern England not from above or below but from the middle [10]. However, given the different senses in which contemporaries used it, as well as the major differences in wealth and political and religious views that divided 'the middling sort', 'the language of sorts' can hardly be seen as a totally satisfactory solution to the problem of classifying people who lived in towns and who did not earn their living on the land.

Nor is this surprising; the problems are difficult ones. Although some professional people (doctors, lawyers, and so on), great officeholders and important merchants had wealth at least equal to that possessed by great landowners, ought one to treat them together in the same category as 'gentlemen'? Similarly, although some tradesmen and craftsmen were as wealthy as yeomen and husbandmen farmers, were they of equal status? There can be no simple answers to these questions. The distinctions between landed and non-landed social groups were much less clear-cut before 1750 than in British society in the nineteenth and twentieth centuries. As will be seen, much manufacturing was carried on in the countryside by people who were also farmers and farmworkers; dual (sometimes multiple) occupations were common. Clearly there are also dangers in exaggerating the distinction between landowners, farmers, merchants, officeholders and professional people. The sons of yeomen farmers were often apprenticed to merchants. Landowners frequently invested money in trade and industry and allowed their younger sons to become lawyers, doctors and clergymen. Successful merchants and professional people, in turn, bought country estates and adopted the life-styles associated with gentlemen landowners.

However, there are good reasons for classifying landed and non-landed groups separately. To do otherwise would be to obscure the growing social importance of the latter. Among the mass of people the dual economy was by no means ended by 1750, but it is highly likely that in the preceding two centuries there was a slow but persistent trend for dual occupations to become less common and for tradesmen and craftsmen to emerge in society as distinct groups. Similarly, the ties between land, trade and the professions remained significant, but landed gentlemen sought (increasingly) to differentiate themselves from those whose wealth was not primarily landed. Whether merchants could become gentlemen was a matter of debate even in the sixteenth century. By the later seventeenth and early eighteenth centuries hostility between the 'landed interest' and 'monied interest' had major political repercussions and the term 'squire' evolved to distinguish landowners from the 'pseudo-gentry' of the towns [14]. Landowners felt themselves to be a distinct social group and it would be unwise of historians to overlook that perception, which was a symptom of the growing importance of mercantile, financial and professional groups in English society by the mid-eighteenth century.

2 GEOGRAPHICAL MOBILITY

As the most perceptive contemporary social commentators, like Smith, Harrison and Wilson, realised early modern England was characterised by much upward and downward social mobility. It is only relatively recently, however, that historians have discovered that this was paralleled by a high degree of geographical mobility. Villages in pre-industrialised England were not close-knit communities inhabited by people who rarely moved from their place of birth. In the centuries before the Industrial Revolution most English men and women migrated from their homes at least once during their lives. That this was not a phenomenon particular to certain regions only became clear in the 1960s when those attempting a large-scale exploitation of parish registers with the aim of reconstructing the population history of the whole country, came across a major problem: in many parishes when baptismal registers were compared with marriage and burial registers, it was found that individuals and often whole families had 'disappeared'. This was a symptom of large-scale internal migration and historians working on a wide range of source material have confirmed the picture of the population of early modern England continually on the move [25–7].

This is by itself an important feature of English society, but it raises numerous historical questions. How far did people move? Where did they move to? Why did they move? Were there any changes in the pattern of population mobility over time? At present it is possible to answer the first two of these questions with more confidence than the last two. Short-distance migration was more common than long-distance. The bulk of the people looked at in all local studies moved only five or ten miles [149]. Long-distance migration did take place but was mainly restricted to the social groups at each extreme of the social spectrum, the very rich and the very poor. Land-owning gentlemen, merchants and professional people frequently travelled to London to pursue their legal, educational, political and social ambitions. Landless labourers and young people travelled long distances in search of work. Not all of this second group moved long distances – adolescent 'servants in husbandry' for example [210] – but some did, especially when hired as day-labourers at hiring fairs. Indeed some labourers spent much of their lives travelling and were separated by a very thin line from the vagrants, who tramped many miles throughout the length and breadth of the country [*Doc. 26*]. Twenty-two per cent of the vagrants who passed through early seventeenth-century Salisbury had already covered at least 100 miles [349]. Some poor migrants even went beyond the shores of England and emigrated to Ireland and the new southern colonies of North America as indentured servants, a step which was merely a logical extension of the mobile life-style of many of the labouring classes of early modern England [27].

The focus of most migration, however, was not the colonies. There were three more important directions of population movement. The first was rural-urban migration. All pre-industrialised towns relied on immigration to maintain and increase their populations, since none had birth rates higher than death rates. By virtue of its size, London was the most powerful magnet for migrants. In the 1550s, 1,060 men whose places of origin are known became citizens of London. Of these only 17 per cent were born in the capital [276]; while in the seventeenth century about one in eight English people visited London at some time in their lives [278]. The second main direction of movement was from 'fielden' to 'forest' areas, the explanation of which lies in the differing characteristics of these areas which will be explained later [*pp. 14–18*]. Finally, overlying these patterns, was a general movement from the north and west of England to the south and east. There is a slight possibility that this is an optical illusion resulting from the fact that most studies have been done of communities in the south and east of England. Studies of northern towns and villages might show migrants originating from the south and east. Until these are done, however, the present evidence is of a drift to the south and east, a trend which fits the unequal geographical distribution of wealth in England that has been commented on above.

It is harder to generalise about the motives for migration than it is to establish the patterns of population mobility, partly because motives for moving surely varied from individual to individual and the vast majority of these are unrecorded. It must be assumed that at least some of the reasons people moved are rooted in other characteristics of early modern English society, which will be discussed in due course. Three of these at least can be mentioned here.

The first is the instability of the English agrarian economy (which will be discussed in the next section) which failed to provide sufficient constant employment opportunities and forced some people to tramp in search of work. The second is the attractions of town life, whether in the form of urban poor-relief schemes or cultural and social opportunities. The third is the pattern of marriage and family customs in early modern England, which ensured that a common feature of the lives of ordinary people was a period during their adolescence which was spent away from the family home. For at least ten years of their lives from the age of about fourteen, many people worked away from home and frequently found marriage partners and a new home there. Sixty per cent of the brides married in the Devon parish of Hartland in the first half of the seventeenth century had been born and baptised in another parish [153]. In Bottesford, Leicestershire, only 6.3 per cent of marriages between 1600 and 1679 were between couples who had been born in the village [90].

The boldest general hypothesis that attempts to explain the scale, type and changes in the pattern of migration is that which begins with the assumption that migrants can be divided into two groups [25]. 'Subsistence' migrants moved because they were compelled to do so by the need to find work and other means of subsistence. 'Betterment' migrants moved, not out of sheer necessity but because of a desire to better themselves. For the period before 1640 subsistence migrants were drawn mainly from the poorer social groups and travelled long distances, often alone. (Bands of masterless people roaming the country begging and thieving were a figment of the frightened imaginations of men of property and authority.) Betterment migrants came from more wealthy families and usually travelled short distances, typically often only to the nearest town to serve as apprentices. After 1660 it may be that this pattern changed and was turned on its head. Poorer subsistence migrants were now much less likely to move long distances and it was the better-off social groups (aided by transport improvements) who travelled further afield.

That is an hypothesis that awaits confirmation. Like many other characteristics of the society of early modern England, all questions about the nature of its geographical mobility are far from resolved. However, the remaining doubts and uncertainties ought not to obscure the certainty that 'migration was not the exception but the social and demographic norm, indeed the usual way of life in early modern England' [26 *p.* 72].

3 AN AGRARIAN SOCIETY

That early modern English society was mobile both from the point of view of movement up and down the social scale and physically about the countryside points to a difficult question that will ultimately have to be faced: was there a change in the basic structure of society between 1550 and 1750? However, before looking in Parts 2 and 3 at the social changes that were taking place, it is important to stress that in many respects English society remained constant throughout these two centuries. The most obvious of these enduring features is its predominantly agricultural economic base. England remained an agrarian society until well into the nineteenth century. Even as late as the 1851 census most English people were engaged in agricultural occupations. Throughout the early modern period only a minority in England did not live or work on the land. Despite criticisms of aspects of Gregory King's work, there is no reason to doubt that his calculation that 74 per cent of English people in 1688 lived in villages, hamlets and farms is an accurate indication of the proportion of people who worked in occupations connected with farming [18; 342].

Because agriculture so dominated its economic and social life early modern England has certain characteristics in common with Third World countries which have 'underdeveloped' economies and societies with a large number of peasant farmers producing food and cloth for subsistence needs. Three of these can be highlighted here.

The first is the chronically unstable nature of the economy which was extremely vulnerable to natural disasters, like outbreaks of epidemics and excessive rainfall. Anything that affected the quality of the harvest in any one year had serious effects on the standard of living of the mass of the people [Doc. 4]. The realisation of this led W. G. Hoskins to conduct a major survey of the quality of every harvest between 1480 and 1759, categorising each on a six-point scale: 'abundant', 'good', 'average', 'deficient', 'bad', and 'dearth', which he determined by the levels of wheat prices in each harvest year [38]. More recently, a more ambitious exercise has been attempted using a price index based on yearly averages of barley and oats as well as wheat prices in order to assess the quality of the harvests between 1465 and 1634 [35]. This has not seriously affected Hoskins's broad conclusions that the harvest failed frequently in early modern England (over the whole period 25 per cent of the harvests were 'deficient', and over 16 per cent 'bad') and that 'deficient', 'bad' and 'dearth' years were often lumped together. The most notable cases are 1527–29, 1549–51, 1554–56, 1594–97, 1646–50, 1657–61, 1673–4, 1692–3, 1695–8, 1708–11, 1727–8, and 1735–40. All this underlines the point that (as in modern underdeveloped countries) the harvest was 'the heartbeat of the economy' and when it failed it shook the foundations of society.

Secondly, also as in many underdeveloped countries, underemployment was a common feature of life. By its very nature agricultural employment is not constant throughout the year. R. H. Tawney, for example, found that in China in the 1930s the typical peasant spent only 100 days working on the land and it is likely that this provides a rough guide to the scale of underemployment in early modern rural England [208]. Thirdly, as in modern underdeveloped countries, poverty was widespread. A common definition of 'underdevelopment' used by economists is the failure to provide acceptable levels of living to a large proportion of a country's population with resulting rising and material deprivation. Recent research suggests that overly gloomy assessments of agricultural production in early modern England need to be qualified, but that ought not lead historians to succumb to any romantic ideas of 'merrie England', where life was one of agrarian contentment. The reality was different; King calculated that over 50 per cent of the population was 'decreasing the wealth of the country' and so was dependent at times on private and public poor relief. This and other contemporary comments [*Doc. 15*] are salutary reminders not to veer too far in an optimistic direction when describing living standards in early modern England [342].

However, there are persuasive arguments against developing the parallel with the agrarian societies of Third World countries in ways that some economists and sociologists have sought to do. For one thing it is highly likely that English agriculture in the early modern period was much more successful in raising its output to meet the needs of an expanding population than might be expected of an 'underdeveloped' country [*Doc. 5*]. This conclusion has been reinforced by recent work on the structure of the English population in this period. Until recently Gregory King's statistics were thought to reflect accurately the major demographic characteristics of early modern England, especially that the numbers of people who were too young or too old to work at full productive capacity (the jargon for this is 'the dependency burden') were as high as those in modern underdeveloped countries. King's calculations that the young (those in the 0–14 age group) made up nearly 40 per cent of the total population and that the average expectation of life at birth was little above thirty years are not only very different from comparable figures for modern industrialised countries like the United Kingdom and the United States of America, where the percentage of the young is approximately half King's figures and the average expectation of life more than double, but they are very similar to those in countries like India, Ecuador and South Korea just after the Second World War.

However, the Cambridge Group working on English population has made significant revisions to King's figures, suggesting that the numbers of young people in the population were lower (about 31 per cent) and that the average expectation of life at birth was higher (in the upper 30s) [157]. If these are correct, then the 'dependency burden' in early modern England was lighter than in traditional societies. This opens up the possibility that the productive capacity of the English economy, and by implication material conditions of life, ought to be viewed in a more optimistic light than they have been by those who have compared them with those in under-developed countries. This is consistent with much recent work on agricultural history, which has highlighted the responsiveness of English farmers to the need to produce more food by the adoption of new techniques and crops and by regional agricultural specialisation. It is highly likely that by the middle of the seventeenth century England had escaped from the vicious cycle of famines that continued to affect other parts of Europe [40; 53; 150]. Even before 1650 there were fewer 'subsistence crises' in which people died of starvation than in contemporary France – crises of the mid-1590s and the early 1620s in parts of northern England are the only known examples which affected England [142; 152]. And after 1650 there is no doubt that English agricultural production made great leaps forward [39; 42].

Unlike some underdeveloped countries early modern England was not a subsistence, nor solely an agrarian, economy. Many people were engaged in producing goods for the market and not only for their own subsistence. In this sense early modern England was not a 'peasant' society and because the word 'peasant' has associations with a largely subsistence economy it is one to be used with great care, if at all [19]. Students of the economic history of England, who will be familiar with features like agricultural innovations, the growth of London as a food market, developing inland marketing facilities in provincial towns, the proliferation of manufacturing industries, and the diversification and redirection of overseas trade, will need little to convince them that early modern England was not a subsistence economy and had not been since at least the thirteenth century. The wide extent of the use of credit in early modern England underlines the point. Loans to other people made up 13 per cent of the total value of personal effects of people who had just died and which were recorded in 4,650 probate inventories between 1650 and 1720 in the east Midlands and Yorkshire. There was a 'wide diffusion of lending among country people' and 'the peasant proclivity for hoarding gold under the bed was not very pronounced' [37 *p. 108*].

Support for this marked difference between early modern England and modern underdeveloped countries is again provided by those working on the history of the family. The extended family that is common in underdeveloped countries was rarely seen in early modern England. There is now abundant evidence that the typical family was a 'nuclear' one, consisting of parents, their unmarried children and servants. The average size of households was small. These aspects and the 'European marriage pattern' of which they are a part will be discussed later. Their importance here is that they point to a family structure that is much more likely than the extended family to produce a surplus for the market.

The nuclear family came to be the major unit of production in early modern England. In the lives of many people there was no clear divide between farming and manufacturing. In many areas there existed a 'dual' family economy in which, for example, a yeoman, his wife and their children might also be spinners or weavers, producers of knitted stockings, wooden goods like hurdles, leather goods like saddles, shoes or gloves, or metal ore and metal goods. Mainly based on a nuclear family economy and using the great pool of underemployed rural labour there developed in England a system of commercial manufacture producing for a domestic and in some cases (especially woollen cloth) an international market.

4 CONTRASTING COMMUNITIES

Diversity is another keynote of the early modern period. Indeed, as local studies proliferate, so the problem of finding a general analytical framework that takes account of the apparently infinite variety of communities becomes increasingly difficult. One possible solution is to make a distinction between communities along climatic and topographical lines: the wetter, cooler Highland Zone of the north and west of England and the drier, warmer Lowland Zone of the south and east. This is not without its value in that it is consistent with the unequal geographical distribution of wealth in early modern England. Agricultural historians have also suggested a variant of this by making a distinction between different communities based on varying soil types: contrasting the drier, lighter soil areas of western England (centred on the Cotswolds) and eastern England (like the sandy heaths of part of East Anglia) with the wetter, colder, heavier soils of the Midland vales. Certainly this is a distinction which helps to account for the varying pace of agrarian change. New crops and techniques for maintaining a larger sheep population were adopted much more quickly in light soil areas like the Cotswolds and parts of Norfolk and Suffolk, transforming them into prosperous sheep–corn farming communities with an expanding grain and wool output. Much slower was the transformation of heavy soil areas like those in Northamptonshire and Leicestershire from grain-growing to stock-rearing and dairy-farming communities. However, useful as these broad geographical distinctions are, they obscure the fact that different types of communities existed within very small areas.

This is revealed by Dr Joan Thirsk's classification of two types of community of early modern England: first 'open pasture' and 'wood-pasture', and secondly 'mixed farming' communities [43]. As the names imply, the primary distinction between the two is economic and it is one that contemporaries noted by using the terms 'forest', and 'fielden' or 'champion'. 'Forest' communities were those in which the main economic activity was pastoral farming, stock-breeding and fattening (cattle, sheep, pigs or horses) and dairying. As might be expected and as is reflected in the studies that have been done, these were primarily *but not solely* in the north and west of England: the forest of Northamptonshire, Myddle in Shropshire, the Pennine area of Lancashire and Yorkshire, the Peak District of south Yorkshire and Derbyshire, the Forest of Arden, the moorland of Cumbria and Gillingham Forest on the borders of Somerset and Wiltshire [47; 52–3; 62–3; 65–6; 70; 247]. In contrast 'fielden' communities largely followed a mixed farming economy, growing grain in conjunction with large sheep flocks which kept the land well manured. Many of those that have been studied are in southern and eastern England: Terling in Essex, Sherington in Buckinghamshire, Wigston Magna in Leicestershire and the open-field areas of Oxfordshire [36; 50; 56; 73]. There is a clear contrast between, on the one hand, the open-field farming, the communal system of husbandry and the concentration on grain and sheep production by a farmer like Robert Loder in the 'fielden' area of Harwell in Berkshire, and on the other the pastoral farming activities of Henry Best in the 'forest' area of the West Riding of Yorkshire [335; 343].

Yet contrasting communities like these were not always separated by long distances. Indeed, they could be next door to one another and this proved to be the case in many different counties in all parts of the country. The most detailed study of this phenomenon is a reconstruction of three Cambridgeshire villages in the sixteenth and seventeenth centuries, the arable 'fielden' communities of Chippenam and Orwell and the fenland, pastoral village of Willingham [67]. Other historians have found the same contrast within one county's borders: Lincolnshire had its 'fielden' villages in the Wolds and its 'forest pasture' communities in the fens; Norfolk's 'sheep-corn' communities were in the north west and its 'wood-pasture' ones in the south east of the county; the lowland plain and coastal plateau of Durham concentrated on dairy farming, while the upland areas of Teesdale and Weardale followed a quite different type of farming; the same contrast was apparent in Sussex between the heavy wold of the north Sussex Weald and the high and open chalk of the South Downs; south Staffordshire had its 'horn' and 'thorn' districts and both Somerset and Wiltshire were divided into areas of 'chalk' and 'cheese' [68; 71; 128; 136].

What makes this 'fielden–forest' categorisation especially important is that the contrasts between the economies of communities is paralleled by other differences. First, patterns of settlement differed markedly. Sussex is typical in that 'the small nucleated villages along the edge of the Downs contrasted sharply with typical wealden settlements', which were dispersed [128 *pp. 3–4*]. Communities in 'fielden' areas were usually physically-compact villages with only a few outlying farms; whereas settlements in 'forest-pasture' regions were in hamlets and farms scattered throughout large parishes. Also, these contrasting settlement patterns often meant a difference in the extent and tightness of manorial and parochial discipline and ecclesiastical control. Magisterial and ecclesiastical authority was much more effective in compact communities than in large, scattered parishes where there was greater scope for individual freedom and independence. Significantly, the Weald was known as 'the wild' in the seventeenth century. Some historians have developed this particular contrasting aspect by differentiating between 'closed' and 'open' communities depending on whether or not a local large land-owner was resident there or not and so able to exercise his influence on the community [54]. The domination of Bottesford by the Manners earls of Rutland partly explains its contrasting history from that of the nearby 'open' village of Shepshed [90]. There were 'closed' villages in 'forest-pasture' areas, like Rockingham in the Northamptonshire Forest, and 'open' villages in 'fielden' areas – Wigston Magna in Leicestershire is the best-known example [56; 63]. But both are exceptions to the typical pattern of relative freedom in 'forest' areas and tight control exercised by the Church and gentry in most 'fielden' communities.

This is partly why a further difference between the two types of communities is that (as has already been noted) 'forest' areas tended to be a major focus of internal migration. Migrants flocked to the 'forest' parts of Norfolk, the Northamptonshire Forest, the Sussex Weald, the moorland areas of Cumbria, for example. A consequence was that these areas became highly populated and in times of economic crisis were likely to be hit hard. Harvest failures in the mid-1590s undoubtedly bore down very hard on the inhabitants of the overpopulated high moorland of Cumbria, where people died of starvation [47]. Similarly in the early 1620s, 1630s and 1640s crises in the cloth trade and high food prices provoked rioting in Gillingham Forest and other parts of Wiltshire and in the fens of eastern England [247]. The association of disorder with 'wood-pasture' areas noted by contemporaries was partly a symptom of the large influx of migrants into these areas [*Doc. 6*]. Migrants were drawn there not simply by the relative freedom; more importantly, they were attracted by the economic opportunities offered by 'forest' areas. In places like Myddle, for example, between the late fifteenth and early seventeenth centuries over 1,000 acres of land were cleared of forests and settled by migrants [52]. In addition, forest communities offered a greater opportunity than 'fielden' areas for supplementing farming income from by-employment in rural manufacturing.

'Fielden' and 'forest' areas were different in farming practices and incidence of rural manufacturing; patterns of settlement differed, as did the degree of magisterial and ecclesiastical control, the extent of migration and population growth. Can the list of differences be extended? Some have argued that it can, though the evidence for further contrasts is less sound than for those that have already been noted. However, there are some grounds for thinking that popular inheritance customs may have differed in the two types of community. Perhaps the adoption of male primogeniture – the inheritance of all the deceased's property by the eldest son – was more pronounced in 'fielden' areas than in 'forest-pasture' regions where partible inheritance – the division of property among the deceased's children – persisted, largely because the availability of supplementary income allowed small, divided farms to be economically viable [81]. If this were so, then it opens up the possibility that there were contrasts in the social structure of the two types of community, notably that small farmers as a social group endured longer in 'forest' areas, with the result that there were less extremes of wealth and poverty than in 'fielden' communities. Even more exciting is the (as yet tentative) suggestion that these economic and social contrasts were paralleled by cultural differences between 'fielden' and 'forest' areas. There are some grounds for thinking that a traditional communal culture centred on the established Church survived longer in 'fielden' than in 'forest' communities because of the differing extent of official control. Religious dissent, for example, was able to thrive in the large open parishes of pastoral areas where the control of parish churches was weakened by the large size of parishes and by the influx of new ideas brought by migrants [318]. What is even more intriguing (though even less well-established) is the suggestion that these cultural differences may have expressed themselves in a distinctive pattern of political allegiances during the English Civil War. It has recently been suggested by D. Underdown, on the basis of his work on Somerset, Wiltshire and

Dorset, that there was a close connection between regional economic, social and cultural differences and the side people chose to support at the outbreak of the Civil War in 1642. The nucleated villages of the arable downlands of these three counties were fertile areas for the spread of royalism; while parliamentarian commitment was more likely to be found in the wood-pasture regions of the south-west [141].

It has to be said that this is a thesis that takes the differences between early modern English communities further than the evidence allows at this stage. This ought not, though, to lead one to abandon the 'fielden-forest' model. It is, as yet, the most convincing hypothesis to make sense of the bewildering variety of regional contrasts in English society in the early modern period.

5 FAMILY AND KINSHIP

When contemporaries wrote about early modern English society, whether it was Gregory King in his cold, statistical description of England in 1688 or Richard Gough in his warm, affectionate recollection of a small Shopshire village in 1700, they described communities as being made up of families or more accurately households, for all those who lived under a family roof, including dependent servants and apprentices, were considered to be a part of the family [338; 342] [Doc. 7]. It has taken historians of English society a long time to recognise the importance of this fact, but recent work has made up for the long neglect [75; 86]. 'Twenty years ago scarcely anyone bothered about the history of the family', wrote Keith Thomas in 1977, continuing with a pardonable degree of exaggeration, 'today an observer might be forgiven for thinking that in France, in the United States of America and in Cambridge historians study little else' [96]. What conclusions have emerged from recent work about the nature of early modern English families and about relationships within them?

Any answer to that question must be prefaced by a note of caution that the primary sources available to family historians are particularly ambiguous and difficult to interpret. The limitations of taxation records and parish registers as sources for English social history will be considered later and they must be regarded at best as flawed sources for the reconstruction of families in this period. Relationships within families are even harder to discover because, although the sixteenth and seventeenth centuries witnessed a proliferation of diaries, autobiographies and letters, such sources need very careful handling. Letters can reveal more about the conventions of letter-writing than about the real nature of personal relationships. It would be unwise, for example, to assume that the formal style of address often used between husbands and wives denoted coolness between them. Nor are letter-writers, diarists and autobiographers necessarily typical of the population. Reasons for keeping diaries or writing autobiographies vary at any one time, but in the early modern period religious motives were particularly strong. Under the impact of Protestantism people searched their consciences and recorded their thoughts and actions. Clearly not all early modern diarists were so motivated – Pepys hardly comes into this category – but spiritual autobiographies and diaries predominate and therefore reflect only that part of the population most influenced by the religious trends of the period. Above all, most of these sources are biased towards the literate and wealthy and there is no certainty that the family structures and relationships they reflect mirror those of all social groups. Common sense suggests there must have been a variety of family situations in early modern England, determined by different social and geographical origins and by personal temperament.

THE ENGLISH 'MARRIAGE PATTERN'

While recognising both the problems posed by the evidence and the need to take account of a variety of experiences, certain characteristics of the nature of families in early modern England do appear to have received fairly general acceptance. Conveniently, though slightly misleadingly since it applied only to northern and western Europe, the history of the early modern English family fits into what has been termed the 'European marriage pattern' [83]. The basic feature of this pattern is that the nuclear (or stem) family, and not the extended (or joint) family, was the norm. As has been seen, this distinguishes early modern England from 'peasant' societies elsewhere then and later. Normally the only people in most households apart from the husband, wife and young children were servants. Using a variety of types of evidence from the later sixteenth to the early nineteenth centuries it has been estimated that over 70 per cent of households were based on the nuclear family; less than 6 per cent had three generations resident and 29 per cent contained one or more servants [89]. It would be wrong to deny the existence of extended families in this period. Clearly they did exist in certain regions at certain times and among certain social groups. Conditions in 'forest-pasture' areas were especially conducive to their formation in that younger sons were not under as much pressure as elsewhere to leave home; in Ryton in Durham the difficult conditions of the 1590s prevented children from leaving home and setting up separate households [76]. Without doubt the households of wealthy landowners were large, being not only domestic establishments but also the political and social centres of magnate power and influence. Yet easily the most typical situation is that found in Ealing in 1599 where the mean household size was 4.75, which is now widely accepted as the norm in early modern England. Although this figure conceals many variations, it is becoming clear that households in early modern England were much smaller than many have thought.

Equally certainly the average age at which people married for the first time was much later than has been commonly assumed. Inherent in the 'European marriage pattern' was the custom that couples did not get married until they could set up an independent household. Until then many adolescents and young adults spent their lives working away from home as servants and apprentices. This has been well documented for those who served annual contracts as farm servants ('servants in husbandry'), and who moved on each year to different employers [210]. Here, as in other aspects, the family life of Ralph Josselin, the vicar of Earl's Colne in Essex, is typical [92]. His children left home in their early teens. This is consistent with a mass of evidence which suggests that for both sexes marriage usually took place in the mid- and late twenties. Statistics from ten parishes between 1550 and 1749 show that the mean male age at marriage fluctuated from 27.1 to 28.1 and the equivalent female age at marriage from 24.8 to 27.0 [153]. As others have pointed out, mean figures like this conceal important variations over time, from place to place and between different social groups. Both for men and women the age at first marriage rose slightly between the late sixteenth and early eighteenth centuries [157]. Short-term variations were more dramatic, especially in periods after mortality crises when the average age at which people married tended to drop sharply because of the unusual opportunities that existed for couples to take over vacant farms and workshops. There were also important geographical variations. The average age at first marriage may have been lower in sixteenth-century Lancashire, while in London native-born girls married significantly earlier than migrant female servants [259; 320]. Earlier marriages were also more common among the children of the land-owning classes and among the daughters of London merchants, whose marriages were often arranged primarily for economic reasons. But the mass of English people who married did so fairly late in life and this is reflected in a mobile adolescent population serving as farm servants or apprentices until well into their twenties.

The late average age at which people married was determined largely by the limited opportunities that existed to set up independent households. This led to another feature of the early modern English family system, which is that a large percentage of people never married at all (in the jargon, the 'nuptiality rate' was low). Typical again was Ealing in 1599, where one-quarter of the women in the 40–70 age bracket were single [88]. It may be that in the early modern period the percentage who never married rose, but the rate was always significantly higher than in modern Britain [157].

Another significant difference from Britain in the nineteenth and twentieth centuries and also from early modern France is that the illegitimacy rate was much lower [80]. Why this should have been, especially given the late age at first marriage, is difficult to explain, apart from seeing it as a result of the successful opposition to extramarital sex enforced by the Church courts and rigidly imposed by communal sanctions [85]. One other possibility is that the low level of extramarital sexual activity is more apparent than real, resulting from the under-recording of infanticide and abortion. That both took place is not in doubt, but it seems unlikely that either could have escaped being recorded on a large scale. There seems little doubt that Peter Laslett's figures (which show that only twice, in the 1590s and early 1600s and in the 1740s, did the illegitimacy ratio rise above 3 per cent) are a reasonably accurate indication of the prevailing pattern of the illegitimacy rate in early modern England [87]. Nor did London have a distinctive pattern. Indeed illegitimacy rates in the capital may have been lower than in rural England [259]. There were temporary sharp rises in illegitimacy rates but these can be explained by the fact that cohabitation was commonly practised outside marriage only by couples who were betrothed and who then probably considered themselves to be married. It was not until Lord Hardwicke's Act in 1753 that the Church wedding service was legally enacted as a necessary part of the process of getting married. Consequently, in the early modern period bridal pregnancy was common [82]. Between 1550 and 1599 in twelve widely scattered parishes the number of babies born within eight months of marriage was 255 per 1,000 and that figure fell only slightly in the seventeenth century, to 228 per 1,000 between 1600 and 1649 and 162 per 1,000 between 1650 and 1699. In these circumstances the time between conception and the finalisation of the marriage was crucial, since if circumstances changed and the marriage was not completed, then clearly the illegitimacy rate would rise. This is what seems to have happened in the late 1590s and early 1600s, which was an atypical period of high illegitimacy rates everywhere. In Terling in Essex there were eighty-two illegitimate births between 1570 and 1699. Of these, twenty-seven took place in the decade after 1597, significantly after the run of bad harvests from 1594 to 1597, which probably disrupted many marriage plans [73].

The final major features of the 'European marriage pattern' stem from the high incidence of mortality in the early modern period, so that death affected family life much more frequently than nowadays. Not only was the duration of marriages shorter and re-marriage more common, but infant mortality was very high and couples had fewer children who survived to adulthood. These facts have suggested to some historians that the relationships between members of the family must have been similarly different. This points to an aspect of family history that is much more contentious than the general structure of the early modern family outlined above, which has received widespread (if not universal) acceptance.

RELATIONS BETWEEN MEMBERS OF THE FAMILY AND KINSFOLK

There has been no shortage of bold, sweeping hypotheses to explain the nature of relationships within the early modern family and between kin. The most popular of these is based on the assumption that many characteristics of the early modern family, especially the short duration of marriages and high infant mortality, weakened relations between members of the nuclear family who were consequently inhibited from making close emotional ties with spouses or children who were soon to be torn from them by death. Marriages were made for practical considerations and usually arranged by parents, rather than for love and by the couples themselves. Relations between husbands and wives and parents and children were cool and harsh. Only with the advent of Puritanism did there begin a slow change in this situation. Puritans stressed the importance of individualism and a by-product of that, it was thought, was a growing respect for individuality, which eventually led to the decline of arranged marriages and the growth of love and affection as a major bond between husbands and wives and parents and children.

The most detailed exposition of this general thesis is by Lawrence Stone [96]. Forceful and persuasively written as his book is, there are strong grounds for questioning its thesis that broad changes were taking place in the history of the early modern family [86]. For one thing, as has been noted, the source material is open to mis interpretation. The conclusion that relations were cool between individuals in the earlier part of the period may reflect the character of the source material rather than reality. The impact of Puritanism on family relations, too, needs to be questioned in the light of recent work which shows that Puritan conduct books advising mutual help and companionship in marriage were far from new [78; 97]. Above all, treatises and conduct books laying down advice on what family relationships should be are no sure guide to what actually was the case.

The principle that was held up by moralists as the foundation of family life was patriarchalism: that only heads of family had independent power and therefore that wives were totally subservient to husbands, and younger brothers and sisters, children, servants and apprentices were all dependent on the head of the household until they married and set up an independent establishment [94] *[Doc. 8]*. Without any doubt this ideal was matched to an extent in reality. The powers of husbands and fathers were extensive and the position of unmarried adults, especially female unmarried adults, within a family household was particularly uncomfortable. Efforts to secure a marriage for Mary Verney failed and she was con-demned to spend her life in her brother's house at Claydon in Buckinghamshire in a state of 'continued spinsterhood' which 'was viewed as a form of social derogation' [*95 p. 84*].

Yet the patriarchal ideal was not dominant in all spheres of family life. Notable exceptions are found in the making of marriages, and in relations between parents and children and between husbands and wives. Marriages between children of wealthy, propertied parents were commonly, though not universally, arranged in this period. Yet among other social groups young people were given much more choice in their marriage partners than the conduct books allowed, as is seen in many diaries. The evidence of sixteenth-century church court proceedings, too, indicates that 'passionate attachment was a common experience further down the social scale and suggests that the ideal of romantic love was deeply rooted in popular culture' [*86 p. 78*].

Nor is this surprising when (as has been seen) many adolescents spent long periods working away from the close supervision of their parents. This lifestyle gave young people in early modern England a remarkable degree of independence that caused anxious-ridden adults in positions of authority to add adolescents to a lengthy list of social groups (scolding women, sturdy beggars, 'the many-headed monster' of the poor, insubordinate tenants, and so on) that were thought to be subverting the fabric of society. As was the case with many of the perceived threats to the social order, these fears were greatly exaggerated. Adolescents rarely lived up to the image of recklessness and insubordination given them by contemporary moralists; they often conformed to social norms. Low levels of illegitimacy indicate that young people shared widely-held assumptions about sex (or rather the lack of sex) before marriage; and the apprentice boys' riots that marked many Shrove Day holidays in London were significantly aimed not at masters or magistrates, but at social deviants like bawdy house keepers and prostitutes. Yet clearly adolescents were not as totally subservient to adults as the patriarchal ideal would suggest [117–20].

Nor were relations between parents and children always as cool and distant as they are sometimes thought to have been by those who have taken too much notice of contemporary conduct books. The assumption that 'parents could not make the same kind of emotional involvement [in their children] which would be con-sidered appropriate today' is questionable [95 *p. 138*]. It certainly flies in the face of many other examples like Ralph Josselin's close relationship with his children or Adam Martindale's and Simonds D'Ewes's moving accounts of the deaths of their children, as well as the elaborate nature of child burials [336; 341] [*Doc. 10*]. Nor is it consistent with the experiences of Richard Napier, the minister and rector of Great Linford in Buckinghamshire, who was 'a seven-teenth-century astrological physician'. His casebook reveals clients from all social groups who came to him 'grief-stricken because of the deaths of children or because they were barren and could have no more children' [91; 13 *pp. 82–3*]. Relations between husbands and wives, too, were warmer, closer and more equal than some have allowed. Wife-beating and cruelty did take place (as Napier's casebooks show). There was a double standard of morality applied to husbands and wives regarding extramarital sex. But married love did exist at all social levels. Nor were wives always submissive and quiescent. Ralph Josselin frequently made decisions about all kinds of matters in consultation with his wife [92].

This opens up the question of the extent to which women's role and status were in reality as inferior as they were legally and theoretically. This is an area of social history on which much interesting research has been done in recent years. This has made it clear that some women played a more independent role in society than is often thought [102; 107; 115]. Many wives of landowners were estate managers alongside their husbands. Many wives of farmers, labourers and craftsmen had a full role in the family economy [*Doc. 9*]. Many women were able to find employment in later Stuart London [104]. The appearance of women in such diverse guises as moneylenders [37], leaders of riots and disorders [243], holders of parish offices, heads of households [100] and witnesses in civil and criminal court proceedings [113; 109; 110] also tends towards a qualification of the conventional roles assigned to women as 'the weaker vessel'. This may account for an upsurge of panic among men, especially in the later sixteenth and early seventeenth centuries, at a perceived threat to male dominance. Whether or not this deserves to be called 'a crisis in gender relations' is uncertain (compare 99 and Ingram in 110), but there is little doubt that male fears lay behind the publication of satirical literature mocking women, as well as the frequent use in English villages in the later sixteenth and early seventeenth centuries of the ducking stool for scolding women [106; 116]. During the Civil War women played an even more active public role as preachers and petitioners [102; 108; 114], which has persuaded some historians to believe that this period contributed to a long-term improvement in the status of women. However, this is a view that underestimates the conservative reaction at the Restoration against what had happened during the English Revolution. It would be foolish to exaggerate the extent of women's independence. Yet, although male dominance was rarely attacked overtly, historians are uncovering the many ways in which women were able to play far from passive roles in many spheres of private and public life in early modern England [104; 111].

Much work still needs to be done before the nature of family relationships and the position of women becomes clear. There is little doubt, however, that bonds of dependence and affection within the nuclear family remained the most important ties in early modern English society.

6 LOCAL COMMUNITIES AND THE NATION

What were the other major types of social relationship in early modern England? In answering this question one has to remember that people probably felt themselves to be part of, not one, but many different communities or groups. 'It would be unfortunate if historians came to think of men's loyalties in this period in mutually exclusive terms. What we need is a more subtle approach to the overlapping loyalties and identities that men felt' [123; 129 *p. 152*]. What were these 'overlapping loyalties and identities' other than those that people felt for members of their intimate family?

The most obvious of these is relationships with kin beyond the nuclear family. These, however, were of much less significance than might be thought by those who compare early modern English society with underdeveloped countries. In some early modern English villages kinship ties were as weak as in some modern communities. As with most generalisations there are important qualifications that one has to make. Kinship ties were especially important to landowners and merchants, whose concern was to ensure that titles, land and wealth, in the absence of heirs within the nuclear family, descended to kin. Merchants, too, relied on kin for credit. Yet even among these propertied groups the importance of kinship ties can be exaggerated. Landowners often made no crucial distinction between kin and others when constructing and maintaining their patronage networks [172]. For many merchants, too, economic and social relationships were not determined solely by family connections. For Quaker ironmasters like Abraham Darby in the early eighteenth century, for example, credit and mutual help came as much from co-religionists as from members of their families. Kinship ties may have been weaker among propertied people than has sometimes been assumed but the lower down the social scale one goes the weaker the ties become. The prevalence of nuclear households and a highly geographically-mobile population militated against the formation of close kinship ties. Relatively few communities existed in which the majority of people were connected by blood and marriage.

Whether in towns or villages the mass of English people had much closer ties with their neighbours than they had with their wider kin [*Doc. 11*]. In this the Essex vicar Ralph Josselin is probably typical. After his wife and children the neighbourhood around his home in Earl's Colne was the most important of several 'communities' he was part of. Like others he relied on his neighbours for economic aid and comfort in troubled times [92]. This pattern seems to be as true of 'forest' as it is of 'fielden' communities, if Kirkby Lonsdale in Cumbria and Terling in Essex are typical of these types of settlements [19; 73]. The strength of neighbourhood ties in early modern English society is reinforced by the evidence of the importance of the parish in village life, since the parish was the basic unit of local government from the sixteenth century onwards. Both the official poor-relief system and schemes of private philanthropy were administered on a parochial basis. Parochial authorities and neighbours alike were expected to cushion individuals against the effects of poverty and disaster. However, like all relationships in early modern England, the one between neighbours was based on mutual reciprocity; it involved obligations as well as rewards. The most notable obligation was to serve as local government officials, as overseers of the poor or constables of the hundred for example. (It is easy to underestimate the extent of popular participation in parochial and hundredal government in this period [*Doc. 3*].)

An equally important ingredient of good neighbourliness was conformity to accepted standards of morality and behaviour. If the institutional expression of neighbourhood ties was the parish, then one important unofficial reflection of them can be seen in local customs and festivities, many associated with the rural and ecclesiastical calendar. Clearly these had many functions, not least being an opportunity for pure enjoyment. But there is undoubtedly more to them than that. The study of popular customs and ceremonies in England by social historians as opposed to folklorists is still in its infancy in comparison with France, but it is already clear that they were sometimes used to enforce communal orthodox values against those who were felt to be deviants [121; 135]. Those felt to be guilty of adultery and other forms of sexual immorality, for example, became the focus of 'charivari' or 'rough music', in which crowds of local people assembled outside the houses of the 'deviants' and rang bells, rattled pots and pans and shouted to indicate their disapproval [*Doc. 12*]. Sometimes such demonstrations were an organised part of the communal calendar, in which adulterers and other 'deviants' were publicly humiliated by being made to ride in procession along with men wearing animals' horns, bearing placards, etc. Such episodes, though superficially light-hearted and characterised by mocking laughter, had a hidden menace that helped to maintain obedience to communal values. On a less menacing level other popular festivities, like harvest cele-brations (sheep-shearing feasts, harvest homes, hopping suppers) involved the whole community and were an affirmation of the social bonds between neighbours [134] [*Doc. 11*]. Especially important in this respect were the Rogation week perambulations of the parish boundaries, reaffirming the geographical limits of one of the most important types of 'community' in early modern England.

Were these neighbourhood bonds less strong in towns? Certainly this is a common presumption that needs to be considered seriously. The development of 'residential zoning' (rich and poor living in separate parts of towns) and influxes of large numbers of migrants were both factors that prevented the formation of close-knit urban communities. However, communal and neighbourhood ties and ob-ligations were as strong in some London parishes as in rural areas. The process of 'residential zoning' was very slow [275]. Many parishes were tiny and were subjected to close communal control by overlapping jurisdictions of parish ward and guild [272–3]. The incidence of office-holding was high, drawing many inhabitants into the government of parishes and wards. In the London parish of Cornhill in the 1640s, 118 officers were elected to serve a pop-ulation of about 1,800, i.e. one in every sixteen inhabitants of the parish was an officeholder [273]. Whether local community ties were as strong in suburban parishes is doubtful, but clearly it would be rash to assume that bonds of neighbourliness were less strong in towns than elsewhere.

Individuals' identities and loyalties were not restricted to family and neighbourhood. One of the great achievements of historical writing over the last twenty years has been to identify a broader focus of people's loyalties, the county community, as another of the overlapping communities of which people felt themselves to be part [124–5]. Most obviously this was true of the great landed gentry, who habitually referred to their county as their 'country' in their letters and speeches, who chose their marriage partners from all parts of the county, and whose circles of patronage and friendship embraced similarly wide areas. Anthony Fletcher's reconstruction of the county-wide bonds between Sussex gentry illustrates this point well [128]. But the county community was a reality for a wider social group than the gentry. Non-gentry sat on Grand Juries, were witnesses or litigants before the county Quarter Sessions and Assizes, and they participated in county parliamentary elections. Indeed the work of Derek Hirst suggests that the county electorate was much less socially exclusive than was once thought and that it was growing in size [130]. 'These participants [in county affairs] included numerous yeomen and townsmen, even husbandmen, craftsmen and labourers, as well as the gentry' [129 *p. 152*].

There is a danger of assuming that the county community was the only or the most important 'community' in early modern England [131–33]. On the contrary, it was neither; it was less important than the family and has to be considered alongside attachment to other types of 'community', namely family, kin and neighbourhood. What is also certain is that identity with one's county did not always conflict with or preclude a sense of belonging to one's country. When people of all social groups habitually moved about the country and had a common language and set of political institutions this is to be expected. Sir Richard Grosvenor, a Cheshire gentleman, at times used the word 'country' to refer to Cheshire and at other times to mean 'some concept of the common good that transcended pure localism and instead referred to the national community of which the local formed but a part' [123 *p. 48*] [*Doc. 13*]. Was there then a growth of nationalism in the early modern period? This is an (as yet) unanswered question, but it is possible that 'growth' implies too lineal a process. People's awareness of the country and of national political issues in this period seems to have fluctuated in intensity, governed largely by war, rather than to have grown. Certainly, among politically-literate people, consciousness of belonging to a national community may have reached peaks separated by troughs, the high points being the early years of the war against Spain in the 1580s, the period just before 1640 and during the next two decades, during the Exclusion Crisis of 1678–81, and again during the wars against France after 1689.

These social bonds and loyalties to 'communities' of family, kin, neighbourhood, county and country overlapped and were not mutually exclusive. Cutting across them all was patronage or 'good lordship' which was the most pervasive social bond of all in early modern England [*Doc. 14*]. J. E. Neale called it 'an association of self-interest, a mutual benefit society. Members expected their patron to sponsor their interests at court and cast his mantle over them whenever the prestige of his name or the cogency of his recommendatory letters might help' [132 *p. 106*]. As Neale's comment implies, patronage was a reciprocal relationship which was valued as highly by patrons as by clients. Patronage was a symbolic expression – a public display on occasions like funerals or when a landlord was met by tenants and retainers on returning to his estates – of the dependence of others on the 'good lord' and of the extent of his influence and power [172; 175].

Patronage was also highly valued by contemporaries as a source of social stability. Consequently, they were prone to fears that it was declining in importance and they expressed their fears loudly and at length. Some historians have taken these views at face value and seen them as a symptom and a cause of a major transition from a society based on 'feudal' paternalism and good lordship to one based on 'possessive individualism' and 'agrarian capitalism' [136; 193]. However, it is possible that this hypothesis exaggerates the extent of change. Paternal ties between landlords and tenants in the eighteenth century are not unlike those that existed in the sixteenth century [191]. Patronage and deference remained a strong social bond throughout the early modern period.

What is less certain is whether the existence of interrelated family, kin, neighbourhood, county and national 'communities' produced a stable society [254; 257]. As will be discussed later (see Chapter 8) they did not prevent outbreaks of conflict, feuds and litigation among the propertied classes, riots and disturbances and crime. But early modern English society was not inherently more disordered and violent than in modern times. David Hey's conclusion after a close study of Richard Gough's contemporary recollection of seventeenth-century Myddle in Shropshire is that the village 'was no rural paradise, but nor was it unusually violent by modern standards. The stories told by Gough are often of the sort that countryfolk can reminisce about today' [338 *p. 23*]. This is an impression that can be extended to seventeenth-century Essex, where most crimes were thefts and the incidence of interpersonal violence was not markedly greater than it is today [255]. Studies of popular riots tend to support the view that early modern society was one in which violence and disorder were contained. Food riots did not become rebellions either in the countryside or in London. Indeed one of the surprising aspects of early modern English social and economic history is that, given periodic outbreaks of economic crisis, rapid inflation before 1650 and great disparity in the distribution of wealth, there were no popular rebellions in England after 1550. This phenomenon and the reasons for it will be discussed later (see Chapter 8). Here it is sufficient to note that the existence of overlapping 'communities' and the persistent strength of deference were ingredients of stability in early modern English society.

Yet stability ought not to be read as a synonym for a fixed and unchanging society. What follows is concerned with outlining the major changes in material conditions and ideas that occurred within early modern English society.

PART TWO: CHANGING MATERIAL CONDITIONS

7 POPULATION FLUCTUATIONS AND CHANGING SOCIAL FORTUNES

Few would doubt that the principal determinants of the major social changes taking place in early modern England were associated fluctuations in the levels of population and prices [*Docs. 15, 16*]. The balance between population and available resources is crucial in determining standards of living in any country at any time. Since changes in that balance in early modern England could not fail to have had a major impact on the material conditions of the mass of people, it is essential that an analysis of changes in early modern English society begins with a discussion of population and price fluctuations. Recent important work (which will be discussed in the next section) has now made it clearer than ever before that the demographic context changed dramatically in the middle of the seventeenth century, dividing the early modern period into two (roughly) equal parts: the first, running from the early sixteenth century, a phase of rising population and price inflation, and the second, ending in the mid-eighteenth century, one of population and price stability. Succeeding sections will be concerned with assessing the impact of this changing demographic and price context on the material conditions of the various groups in English society which were identified in Chapter 1.

As might be expected, historical investigation of this subject has revealed a bewildering variety of individual experiences, which makes the task of generalising about the fortunes of each social group very difficult. A much greater problem, however, is that of discovering a general pattern of change taking place in early modern English society as a whole. Undoubtedly there is room for many different general interpretations. One that has received strong support from some social historians is that of 'social polarisation', a polarisation of both wealth and of culture. It has been argued that not only did some people grow richer in the period of demographic expansion and inflation of the sixteenth and early seventeenth centuries but also that the gap between rich and poor became wider. So entrenched was this pattern of enhanced inequality in the distribution of wealth by the mid-seventeenth century that the changed demographic and price context of the later seventeenth and early eighteenth century failed to alter it. 'Demographic stabilization and economic growth eased the tensions generated by the process of economic polarization, though without reversing its outcome' [3 *p. 228*]. Successful, prospering groups like large farmers, merchants and other 'middling' groups gradually drew closer to the large landowners of England and distanced themselves from the mass of labouring poor. This economic and social polarisation, it is believed, was paralleled and reinforced by a process of cultural polarisation. The major religious and intellectual ideas of early modern England were absorbed by the educated 'patrician' upper and middling groups in society, whereas the 'plebeian' labouring poor remained illiterate and ungodly [3; 307].

It is possible that this 'social polarisation' theme presents too stark and pessimistic a view of the nature of social change in early modern England. It would be wrong, of course, to claim that this was any other than a society in which wealth was distributed very unequally. Moreover, it is also true that the Price Revolution of the first part of the period favoured some social groups more than others. Taken as a whole the land-owning classes, larger farmers, manufacturers, merchants and professional groups undoubtedly prospered; while at the same time some small farmers found it difficult to survive and for labourers who relied largely on wages for their incomes, standards of living fell drastically. But, as will be seen, there are many qualifications that must be made to this analysis of 'social polarisation'. Not all small farmers by any means were forced off the land in the period before 1650. Nor were labourers a homogeneous group whose economic fortunes universally deteriorated. The scale of agricultural progress in the sixteenth and early seventeenth centuries appears to have been sufficient to enable England to escape the frequency of subsistence crises that hit other parts of Europe including France before 1650. The economic divide between rich and poor may not have become as starkly clear-cut by the mid-seventeenth century as the proponents of the 'social polarisation' hypothesis assume.

What is more certain is that after 1650 prosperity was diffused more rapidly and more generally throughout English society than ever before as a direct consequence of the new demographic and price context, combined with accelerating agricultural productivity.

It is important, of course, not to paint too optimistic and prosperous a picture of English society in the later seventeenth and early eighteenth centuries. The bedrock of poverty and squalor at the base of society persisted. Faced with falling grain prices, smaller farmers found the going tougher even than in the previous century, and lesser landowners suffered from declining rent-rolls as the demand for tenancies fell. Larger landowners and farmers were able to use their greater economic reserves to cushion themselves against these harsh economic currents and to invest in potentially profitable innovations. The period, therefore, saw an accelerated trend towards a three-decked rural society of large landowners, large farmers and a mass of landless labourers which was unlike the two-decked 'landlord–peasant' society of Ireland, Scotland or France. Yet this pattern of change in landed society was not at all straightforward or clear-cut. Not all lesser landowners and small farmers suffered a decline in material conditions. Moreover, the end of price inflation and population growth put labourers in a much more advantageous position than ever before (or at least since similar conditions in the fifteenth century).

In 1750, by the standards of modern industrialised societies, poverty was still rife and wealth still unequally distributed. But in the previous two centuries (and certainly in the last century) there had taken place a marked percolation of wealth downwards and outwards on an unprecedented scale. It is possible, indeed, to discern the dim outlines of a 'consumer society'. Perhaps, too, this was a society that was characterised by more pluralism and diversity than the 'polarisation' thesis indicates. There is mounting evidence that the traditional view that the process of social change slowed down after 1650 needs revising, and that, on the contrary, the economic progress of the late seventeenth and early eighteenth centuries spawned rapid social changes, especially urbanisation and the growing importance in English society of non-landed elements drawn from middling groups, like craftsmen, merchants, artisans, manufacturers and professional people. To suggest that the relationship of these groups was one of close cultural identification with the upper elite in landed society, so divorcing themselves from 'popular culture', may be misleading, as will be seen. The complexity and diversity of English society by the end of the early modern period is difficult to compress into the tight confines of models of 'social polarisation' and 'cultural differentiation'.

POPULATION TRENDS

Recent work on the population history of early modern England has been dominated by the Cambridge Group for the History of Population and Social Structure, which was founded in 1964 by R. S. Schofield, E. A. Wrigley and P. Laslett. Such has been the success of the Group's publicity [6; 87–9; 153; 156–7] that it is easy to forget that others had already established the broad trends of population movements in early modern England: a long-term rise in population to about the mid-seventeenth century, followed by a century-long period of population stagnation [143–4; 147–8]. Within that broad pattern it was clear that there were sharp short-term deviations, notably a steep drop in the level of population in the late 1550s caused by a series of influenza epidemics.

Further significant advances in knowledge were prevented by the intractability of the available primary sources. No national population census exists for the period before 1801 and the only direct sources for population history are a few community listings usually made by church ministers, like those for Ealing in 1599 and for Clayworth and Cogenhoe in the later seventeenth century. Historians of English population in the early modern period, therefore, have to rely on records made originally for purposes other than estimating and explaining changes in population levels. These are mainly taxation records (parliamentary subsidy returns, especially for the early sixteenth century, and hearth tax returns which exist for the late seventeenth century), assessments for levying men, horses and weapons for the militia (mainly sixteenth century), the returns made of those males who took the Protestation Oath of 1641, and ecclesiastical censuses of communicants of the Church made at various times but principally in 1563, 1603 and 1676 [154]. All of these sources are, of course, listings of some, but not all, individuals living in each community at various periods. Therefore, in order to translate the numbers counted in these documents into totals that approximate to all the inhabitants of each county, multipliers have to be devised to take account of those who were not included in these documents because they were women, young, poor or non-Anglicans, thus introducing a large element of uncertainty in the results.

It was long realised that there was another source – parish registers – that was more comprehensive than these. Parish registers include most individuals at three points in their lives: at baptism, marriage and burial. They were first authorised in 1538 and registers for many parishes begin from the late sixteenth century.

However, they are not without their drawbacks [145]. Many registers contain gaps in the series and those that survive often suffer from under-registration because of inefficient clergy (see the frequent acts and orders, like those in 1653 and 1694, which attempted to remedy this), the gap between birth and baptism, and the existence of non-Anglicans. Furthermore, because there was a highly mobile population (as has been seen), it is very difficult to use parish registers to trace individuals from birth to marriage to death, simply because many moved from the parish in which their baptism was recorded. One therefore needs a block of registers from adjacent parishes to take account of (at least) short-distance migration, and such a block is unlikely to survive. As a result, parish registers are liable to produce records of atypical early modern men and women: those who did not move from their place of birth. But the biggest drawback of parish registers as a source for population history of the whole country is their sheer bulk, given that there are over 9,000 parishes.

The Cambridge Group has made a major attempt to overcome some of these problems by tapping a large reservoir of enthusiastic help from local historians, by skilfully co-ordinating their work and by devising ingenious methods of processing the data drawn from parish registers. In 1981 the Group presented a full statement of these methods in a book by Wrigley and Schofield [157], which sets out the long-term trends in the history of English population during the early modern period more clearly than ever before. In 1550 the population of England (in line with that throughout Europe) was rising fairly quickly. From about 2.3 millions, based on subsidy assessments for 1522–5, it had risen to 2.8 millions by 1541, 4.1 millions by 1601 and 5.281 millions by 1656. This was the peak which marked the beginnings of a dramatic transition to a period of population stagnation and even decline, which lasted for another century. By 1701 the population level had sunk back to 5 millions and had risen only to 5.6 millions by 1741.

Short-term fluctuations within this broad pattern have also been given statistical precision by the Cambridge Group. The lack of parish registers before 1538 makes it impossible to date the exact beginnings of the population expansion after the late medieval phase of population stagnation that was caused, among other things, by the mid-fourteenth-century Black Death. But certainly by the early 1550s the population growth rate was very fast, at about 1 per cent a year. But in the late 1550s there occurred a sharp temporary setback and between 1556 and 1561 the population fell from 3.2

millions to just under 3 millions, a drop of 5.5 per cent. (This is a lower mortality figure than some have found.) There then followed a very high growth rate from 1561 to 1586 of over 1 per cent a year, a rate that was not exceeded until the later eighteenth century. From 1586 to 1601 the growth rate fell to 0.5 per cent a year and in three years (1587, 1591 and 1592) baptisms only equalled burials, and in 1597 burials far exceeded baptisms. The overall growth rate increased slightly in the early seventeenth century (but always remained below 1 per cent) and this was maintained (after a sharpish drop in 1621) until 1656. The next thirty years, however, were a period of stagnation and, even when the population began to grow again from the 1690s, it did so very slowly before 1750, only occasionally rising faster than 0.5 per cent a year.

The most interesting conclusions of the Cambridge Group relate to the major puzzle of why population levels fluctuated as they did. The Group's work may not have solved this puzzle once and for all, but it has clarified the historical debate. One needs, first of all, to make a clear distinction between short-term and long-term population trends. As has been seen, mortality crises periodically punctuated the early modern period and were followed by sharp rises in birth rates until pre-crisis population levels were reached. In an age when causes of death were un- or ill-recorded, the difficulty for the historian is in discovering whether mortality crises were caused by harvest failures and famine or by disease. The two causes could act independently of each other: in Cumbria and Westmorland and parts of Durham and Yorkshire there is convincing evidence that the main cause of widespread mortality between 1594 and 1597 was starvation in the wake of four bad harvests in a row. Similar evidence for Lancashire in 1623 – of burials peaking in December and January when the plague virus was inactive – suggests that another subsistence crisis hit some north-western parishes [47; 142]. Moreover, epidemics were not always linked with bad harvests. In late sixteenth-century London for example, epidemics (mainly bubonic plague) ravaged the population at a time when bread prices were low [158]. Similarly, late seventeenth- and early eighteenth-century mortality crises occurred when agricultural productivity was outstripping demand, suggesting that the prime cause of deaths was diseases like typhus, smallpox and influenza (1434). It is, however, probable that most mortality crises were brought about by diseases hitting a population undernourished after a bad harvest [151; 152], as was the case when an influenza epidemic coincided with bad harvests to produce the severe mortality of the later 1550s [144]. When conditions improved after better harvests and the epidemics had run their course, delayed marriages were contracted and earlier marriages were made possible, because of vacant holdings caused by the previous high mortality. Consequently, a higher than average death rate was followed by an equally temporary sharp rise in the birth rate, a process called by historical demographers 'demographic homeostasis'.

Explanations of long-term population trends have long been the subject of a debate which has centred on the question of whether change in the death-rate or in the birth-rate was the key controlling factor. Until recently long-term changes in mortality have been the most popular explanation, on the assumption that fertility levels were less volatile than mortality levels. The Cambridge Group's conclusions do not challenge this orthodoxy completely. Indeed, their figures suggest that mortality changes are a partial explanation for long-term population changes, since levels of mortality were lower and the average expectation of life at birth higher in the period of population expansion than when population declined after 1650. Why the incidence of mortality should grow and the average expectation of life at birth should fall in the early modern period is not clear. But it is possible that this was caused by diseases operating independently of the economic context. Bubonic plague certainly seems to have been less virulent and largely restricted to towns in the sixteenth and early seventeenth centuries before its final demise in 1665, which may account for falling mortality levels in that period. Rising mortality levels during a time of growing prosperity in the later seventeenth and early eighteenth centuries suggest that non-plague diseases (especially typhus and smallpox) were the key causes.

However, the most dramatic conclusion of the Cambridge Group is that fluctuations in fertility levels were at least equally as important as those in mortality levels in explaining changes in population in early modern England. Changing fertility levels were controlled by two factors: the age at which women married and the proportion of people who married. (The Group has now abandoned its earlier belief, based on Wrigley's work on Colyton in Devon, that fertility was affected significantly by the practice of family limitation methods [155].) As has been seen, throughout the whole period the age at first marriage and the percentage of those who never married were higher than in modern Britain. Yet the Group's figures suggest that both figures tended to move together, and were lower in the period before 1650 than after. In an age when knowledge of contraceptive techniques extended only as far as *coitus interruptus* and prolonged lactation, and since (as has been seen) extramarital sex and illegitimacy were rare, even slight changes either in the numbers who married or in the age at first marriage for women could affect the birth rate significantly. The logic of this is upheld by the Group's estimates of gross reproduction rates, which after rising in the sixteenth century fell during the seventeenth century and rose only slightly in the early eighteenth century, when the age at first marriage and the percentage of people who married both fell slightly again, before the dramatic fall in both figures in the later eighteenth century.

What, of course, is still unanswered is why the age at first marriage and the percentage of people who married should have changed as it did. One intriguing possibility is that both moved in response to economic conditions: that there existed (in the words of J. D. Chambers) 'a population able to recognise economic opportunities when it saw them and ready to adjust marriages and childbearing propensities more quickly, and to a greater extent, than is commonly allowed by those who assume that . . . birth rates were more or less constant at the limit of biological potential' [143 *p. 65*]. If this were so, then it is possible the falling fertility levels of the seventeenth century came about as a result of the determination of men and women to protect and improve their living standards by having small families and preventing population outstripping resources. It could then be argued that fertility levels only rose in the early eighteenth century when men and women considered that economic conditions – whether of flourishing rural industries or of burgeoning agricultural productivity – were sufficiently soundly-based to allow them to marry earlier than had been usual. But that is an argument that is based on even less sure ground than many that have been put forward in this section.

PRICE TRENDS

The historical debate on the course and explanations of price trends in early modern England has not been as lively in recent years as that on the history of population and therefore can be dealt with more briefly. There are close similarities between the historical study of both topics. Price trends, like population trends, have to be reconstructed from inadequate statistics. The best-known price index by Phelps-Brown and Hopkins covers the whole period but is based on prices paid for goods by institutions in southern England, which are not always representative of retail prices or prices paid for goods in all parts of the country. The index also tries to compress all prices into one series using the concept of a 'composite unit of consumables' [161]. Peter Bowden's price indices for 1500 to 1750 are more sophisticated, using a wider range of sources than Phelps-Brown and Hopkins; Bowden also produces price series for a range of individual commodities [159–60].

As a result the major price trends in early modern England are now clear [168]. The price stability of the period from the late thirteenth century ended in the early sixteenth century and was followed by a period of inflation which was (by modern standards) not severe. However, from the 1510s to the 1550s prices rose rapidly: agricultural prices rose by 250 per cent in this period. There then followed (as was the case with population trends) a period of much slower price rises in the early-mid-Elizabethan period. In the 1590s prices again rocketed, but slowed down again in the early seventeenth century. There was another sharp rise in the late 1640s, but the long period of inflation ended in about the middle of the century. From that point onwards for about a century the long-term trend of prices was slightly downwards. Again this trend conceals short-term variations; for example the Phelps-Brown and Hopkins index rises sharply and temporarily in the early 1710s and early 1740s. The contrast between the price context before and after 1650 is the most striking aspect of these price trends. Another important feature, however, is the contrast between movements of food and industrial prices. Before 1650 food prices rose much quicker than industrial prices; whereas after 1650 food prices fell more rapidly than industrial prices. Indeed, Professor Coleman's re-working of Phelps-Brown and Hopkins's figures suggests that industrial prices did not fall at all after 1650 but continued to rise slowly [33].

Although they have not occasioned as much recent interest, just as much uncertainty surrounds the explanations for these trends as for population fluctuations. From the earliest work on the subject by J. Thorold Rogers [169] down to the 1950s, monetary explanations for the Price Revolution of the sixteenth and early seventeenth centuries held the field, especially the debasement of the coinage by Henry VIII's government and the influx of bullion from the silver mines of the New World to England via Spain. However, the fact that the period of inflation began well before either of these events, together with other considerations, caused these monetary theories to be rejected, especially when it became clear that they did not explain the different movements of food and industrial prices. It would, of course, be foolish to reject monetary explanations altogether, since European silver was being produced in increasing quantities between 1460 and 1530 [161], and Challis has discovered that Spanish silver was held in the Mint in the Tower in the few years for which records survive in the later sixteenth century [162]. An increase in silver bullion supplies cannot be ruled out completely as a possible cause of the Price Revolution. Moreover, the currency manipulations of Henry VIII's government contributed directly to the rapid inflation of the 1540s, and the subsequent currency reform by Elizabeth I and her ministers is a partial explanation for the slackening price inflation of the mid-Elizabethan period [163–4; 166].

However, some historians have felt for many years that monetary theories do not get to the heart of the puzzle of explaining price movements. The result has been that most historians of prices place more weight on 'real' factors, i.e. explaining price trends in terms of population movements. It is argued convincingly that the growing population throughout the sixteenth and early seventeenth centuries produced a demand for food that outstripped supply, resulting in a rapid rise in food prices. Industrial prices, on the other hand, were less prone to rise, because, although the prices of industrial raw materials might go up, the main manufacturing cost was labour and the rise in population ensured that wages costs and therefore industrial prices were kept low. The same kind of argument, moreover, fits the situation after 1650 equally neatly. Since population pressure slackened off and agricultural productivity increased, so food prices fell fairly rapidly. Prices of manufactured goods, however, continued to rise, largely because the labour supply was less abundant; as a result, wages rose and with them manufacturing costs, which were reflected in higher-priced industrial goods.

There is an additional possible explanation for the peculiar continued tendency of industrial prices to rise throughout the early modern period and especially after 1650. This is that after 1650 the demand for industrial goods grew and ensured that, despite both a falling population and lower prices for industrial raw materials, prices of manufactured goods were kept high. On this point, however, the debate on the causes of price trends spills over into the subject of the rest of this chapter: the changes in material conditions of early modern English men and women.

'GENTLEMEN': THE GROWTH AND CONSOLIDATION OF THE LAND-OWNING CLASSES

The economic fortunes and subsequent social changes affecting the English land-owning classes during the early modern period have been the focus of as much heated controversy as any historical problem that one can think of. Until very recently much of the debate was concerned with the century before 1640, and comparatively fewer historians discussed what happened to land-owners during the later seventeenth and early eighteenth centuries. During the last few years, however, there has been a marked shift of interest by historians towards the later period.

For a long period after the end of the Second World War some of the best historians in Britain and America were obsessed with attempting to clarify the major social changes taking place among the English landed elite in the century before the Civil War. It can hardly be said that they succeeded. The 'storm over the gentry' was not short of clear, bold and exciting theses, of which the first and best was the one that inspired the debate, by R. H. Tawney, but most of them contradicted each other [194; 196]. The 'storm' ended in 1965 with the publication of Lawrence Stone's 'blockbuster' of a book, an analytical study of every major aspect of the lives of the Elizabethan and early Stuart peerage [193]. Its central thesis is that peers as a group underwent a major economic crisis in the later sixteenth century, from which they recovered in the early seventeenth century only by adopting hard-headed estate policies. As a result they recovered their economic position, but at the expense of alienating their tenants. In this and other ways their social and political influence was eroded and they were forced into a damaging alliance with the Crown against the gentry. Their economic crisis of the later sixteenth century was thus followed by an even greater political crisis in the early seventeenth century.

The book got the kind of lengthy reviews it deserved, most of them praising the breadth of vision of its argument but questioning its statistical and evidential bases. Yet curiously these criticisms were not pursued and at that point the debate fizzled out. After the publication of Stone's book the study of the English landed elite became unfashionable for over a decade, a period during which social historians instead focused their attentions on the mass of people and not just on the tiny elite at the apex of society. The beneficial fruits of this shift of interest 'from peers to peasants' will be seen later, but one adverse effect of it was to leave the study of the English land-owning classes before 1640 in an unsatisfactory state. All that had been shown was that landed fortunes were fluid and changing; beyond that 'the storm over the gentry' had produced no agreed pattern of social change.

Until very recently studies of English landownership in the century after 1640 could hardly have been more different. They were largely dominated by the work of one historian, H. J. Habakkuk, whose interpretation of the period was almost universally accepted [185; 188]. Coincidentally, the essentials of Habakkuk's view were published at exactly the same time as Tawney's work on the earlier period. However, unlike Tawney's thesis, Habakkuk's attracted little controversy and the work of a small band of scholars gave it strong support [191]. Moreover, in contrast to the apparent mobility and uncertainty characterising landownership before 1640, Habakkuk's orthodox view of the later period was one of social stability, appropriate to an age of Augustan calm and burgeoning political stability. He portrayed a clear drift of property away from smaller landowners into the hands of wealthy ones, where it stayed.

Paradoxically, the effect of research during the last decade or so has been to bring clarity to the question of social changes affecting landowners in England in the century before 1640 and to plunge the same question in the period after 1640 into controversy and uncertainty.

1550–1640

Two major criticisms can be levelled against Stone's 'crisis of the aristocracy' argument. The first is that his use of evidence to support it is open to doubt. Inevitably much of this kind of criticism is technical and in 1972 Stone hit back spiritedly at some of his critics for 'chewing away on these dry old bones', but it is important to note the many serious doubts some historians have had regarding the evidence on which Stone rests his thesis. In view of these, Stone's case that the peerage as a whole suffered a great loss of income in the late sixteenth century must be considered at best as not proven. So too must his assumption that the 'aristocracy' and 'gentry' were two distinct social groups with contrasting economic fortunes. The distinction between peers and gentry is primarily a legal, not an economic, one. There were differences among the English land-owning classes, but they were based on the possession of estates rather than titles of honour. It was differences in wealth which set apart the 'county' magnates from the lesser 'middling and parochial' gentry and which determined that the former would become deputy lieutenants, justices of the peace, and county members of parliament; while the latter often had to settle for less prestigious offices. These differences are accurately reflected in the terms contemporaries used to describe themselves and others: knights, esquires, gentlemen and (from 1611) baronets. However, as has been noted, these differences are less important than the gulf which separated all of them (titled and non-titled, lesser and greater landed gentlemen) from the rest of landed society. They were united by the fact that they possessed sufficient income (the bulk of which came to them as landlords from rents and entry fines) to maintain a life-style which accorded with contemporary descriptions of gentility based on leisure and responsibility. Gentlemen (whether peers or commoners) were those who had sufficient wealth to give them the independence and freedom to devote themselves to serving the commonwealth [*Doc. 3*].

If that wider social group of landed gentlemen (including the titled peerage but excluding those whose income was not sufficient to give them leisure and independence) is looked at, then it becomes clear that the first major social change that it underwent in the century after 1540 is a great growth in its wealth and its size [*Docs. 17, 18*]. Estimates of the size of this group in the counties that have been studied are not directly comparable, because some historians take the possession of coats of arms as the main indicator of gentility, while others (perhaps more wisely) have included all those who were called 'gentlemen' by contemporaries. However, clearly in county after county this group became larger and larger and wealthier and wealthier [126–7; 179; 182]. In 1436 the class of 'gentlemen' held 40–45 per cent of land in England; by 1690 it held 60–70 per cent. There seems little reason to doubt that the later sixteenth and early seventeenth centuries (especially the period 1580–1620) 'saw a massive redistribution of income in favour of the landed class . . . the social class of the landowner – whether gentry or aristocracy – was of seldom more than marginal significance. In general . . . the prosperity of the landowner in Tudor and early Stuart times must have depended much less upon his social origins than upon the nature of the land which constituted his estate and its sensitivity to economic change' [159 *p. 695*].

Why was the century before 1640 one of great prosperity for landed gentlemen? This cannot be answered without recognising that there were conditions peculiar to the period that gave some large landowners (regardless of the individual's abilities) economic problems. This was a period in which the social pressures on those with wealth to display it by spending money were great. Fortunes were poured into building grand houses, providing lavish hospitality and scrambling after outward signs of gentility like coats of arms and long (sometimes bogus) family trees. Such 'conspicuous expenditure' did not pass without contemporary comment [*Doc. 19*]. Expenditure on litigation was also heavier than at other times in this period, not simply because landowners were inevitably drawn into property disputes, but because the land law regarding the descent of property was going through a period of temporary uncertainty. Consequently, it became very difficult for landowners to devise settlements which ensured the descent of their entire estates for more than one generation. These circumstances fostered inheritance disputes and forced landowners to spend vast sums in litigation or on extra-legal settlements [183]. Unfortunately for landowners, the state of the law regarding credit was also inimical to their interests. Landowners were always in debt, not because they were in serious financial difficulties but because their rental income fluctuated and they often needed to borrow large capital sums to finance expensive projects like house-building. The law in this period presented peculiar dangers to debtors, especially to those who borrowed on mortgages. Late sixteenth- and early seventeenth-century courts very readily gave judgments against defaulting debtors, to the great advantage of London merchant-financiers like Thomas Sutton, Arthur Ingram and Lionel Cranfield in the early seventeenth century. It was not until the middle of the seventeenth century that the principle of equity of redemption evolved as a protection for debtors against such judgments.

It would, however, be wrong to exaggerate the impact of these problems on the economic fortunes of the land-owning classes, who had resources large enough to absorb most of the costs involved. Moreover, the problems were easily outweighed by economic and political aspects of the century before 1640 from which most landowners were able to profit. First of all, contemporary demographic and price trends could not but help large landowners to run their estates profitably. Their estates were their principal source of income. Opportunities for court office were very limited in this period and, although investment in trading and industrial ventures and urban development became fashionable, few made large profits from it. Landowners relied primarily on income from farming, selling timber, exploiting mineral resources on their estates and, above all, on rent. In this respect their main problem was to ensure that their rental incomes were not eroded by the Price Revolution.

This was a problem that most overcame [177]. There were, of course, landowners who did not, either because they were incompetent estate managers or because their estates were let out on conditions which secured their tenants against demands to pay more rent. As will be pointed out later in this chapter, some tenants did have greater legal security than was once thought. But in many cases landlords in the later sixteenth and early seventeenth centuries were able to use new surveying techniques to gather information about their estates with which they were able either to persuade tenants to pay new commercial rents ('rack rents', which were not necessarily inequitable) or to change customary tenures with low annual rents and high entry fines into short leasehold tenures with realistic commercial rents. More often than has been realised, however, such techniques by landlords were not necessary. As a result of the rapidly rising population and food prices of the period demand for tenancies was inevitably high, and it may have been this fact that was more responsible for pushing up the level of rents than the machinations of 'covetous' landlords [*Doc. 24*]. Most estates that have been studied show evidence of a marked rise in rental incomes at least in line with the rise in land values and the fall in the value of money.

As well as the economic context, political conditions of late sixteenth- and early seventeenth-century England also helped English landowners to prosper. This was a period when the English land-owning classes were the lightest-taxed elite in the whole of Europe, simply because all attempts by the Crown to reform its inefficient system of public finance before the 1640s failed miserably. It was a system which was built into the political structure of the country. Low taxes were a *quid pro quo* given to the landed classes for their continuing support of the Crown. Large landowners, too, were major beneficiaries of the sales of Crown and Church lands which went on from the Dissolution of the Monasteries in the 1530s for the next century. It is now clear that most ex-ecclesiastical and ex-Crown land that came onto the market in this period was bought by existing (not new) landowners. This fact underlines the predominant trend affecting the elite of landed society in the first half of the early modern period: as the Crown's and the Church's landed estate dwindled, so the share of the land held by a swollen class of landed gentlemen grew.

1640–1750

Life for the landowning classes deteriorated after 1640. The period, of course, began with a major political crisis that escalated into Civil War, army revolt and then a political revolution in the winter of 1648–9. This 'English Revolution' was not followed, however, by a revolutionary transformation in landed society. Fines imposed on their enemies by both sides in the Civil War were not usually ruinous. Many Royalist landowners who had their estates confiscated managed to regain them by buying their lands back or by getting friends and relatives to do this, and after the Restoration there is no doubt that the majority of Royalists successfully regained their land [186–7; 197–8]. Yet the short-term effects of the military and political turmoil of this period on all landowners and especially on those who remained loyal to the king ought not to be minimised. High taxation, fines, confiscation of the estates of 'delinquents' (i.e. Royalists), and the re-purchase of confiscated property forced many landowners to mortgage and borrow heavily. Moreover, the rental incomes of some gentry landowners fell off rapidly during the war years. The impact of the Civil War was much more severe than has sometimes been realised. To Royalist landowners like the eighth earl of Derby what made this situation harder to bear was that at the Restoration in 1660 there was no royal decree or parliamentary statute invalidating enforced sales of lands or compensating those who had suffered in the king's cause during the 1640s and 1650s [*Doc. 20*]. Many landowners emerged in Restoration England with a heavier-than-normal debt load as a consequence of the English Revolution [172; 181; 198].

Moreover, in the period after 1660 landowners had to face continued high taxation, in great contrast to the period before 1640. The parliamentary financial reforms of 1643 were the first successful stage in carrying out a reform of public finance that had been shirked by Elizabeth I and had failed during the reigns of James I and Charles I before 1640. These reforms were not completely overturned after 1660, and during the next century levels of direct taxation reached new heights: after 1689 the land tax was levied at its full 20 per cent rate of four shillings (20p) in the pound in certain southern and eastern regions of England. Above all, rental incomes after 1660 failed to rise on anything like the scale they had before 1640. As food prices fell, tenant farmers found it more difficult to pay rents. As the population stagnated there were no longer large numbers of people waiting to take on new tenancies; complaints of 'decay of rents' abounded, and rents often fell into arrears [184] [*Doc. 21*]. In what was perhaps an extreme case, on the estate of the earl of Middleton in Shropshire a gross annual rental of £2,854 was exceeded by accumulated arrears of rent of £4,941 [191].

Taken together, these circumstances of rising debts and taxation demands and falling rental income were ones which greater landowners ought to have been able to cope with more successfully than smaller ones. They had the security on which to borrow money to cover extremely difficult periods, and the evolution of the principle of equity of redemption made the mortgage a safer method of raising money than it had been before. Large landowners were also likely both to attract wealthy heiresses in marriage and to secure lucrative offices in a state bureaucracy that (as will be seen) was expanding rapidly after 1660 and especially after 1689. All this suggested to Habakkuk that in the later seventeenth and early eighteenth centuries there was probably a drift of lands out of the hands of smaller landowners, ensuring 'the growth of the great estate', especially after his study of a group of estates in Northamptonshire and Bedfordshire showed that landowners were successfully using a legal device, the strict settlement, to ensure that estates would be kept largely intact from generation to generation. Large estates became larger and the land market slowed down as existing large estates secured a cast-iron legal protection against being broken up. This is an idea that has received the support of L. Stone, who (with J. C. Fautier Stone) has argued in another big book on the upper reaches of English landed society that the composition of the landed elite throughout the early modern period remained much more stable than many have commonly assumed [195].

Persuasive as this Habakkuk thesis is, recent research suggests that it cannot be applied everywhere. Sale of land continued apace in eighteenth-century Lincolnshire and there was no marked trend of land into the hands of existing large landowners [190]. Elsewhere in the north east and in Cumbria, for example, there existed a greater diversity than the Habakkuk thesis allows. In Cumbria the land tax was not high and rents were not universally low [178]. Moreover, mortgages (though safer) were still expensive and landowners had to face competition for offices from merchants, professional people and other non-landed social groups. Above all, however, it is Habakkuk's stress on the importance of the strict settlement as a guarantee of stability of large landed fortunes that is questionable. It was not employed to anything like the extent that Habakkuk assumed; it was also much easier to break than he thought; and anyway it was often impossible to use because of the failure of the land-owning classes to replace themselves in this period [184].

The current attack on Habakkuk, though not as vitriolic as that on Tawney a generation ago, is threatening to develop into a latter-day 'storm over the gentry' for this later period and to throw a question that had been clear into confusion. It would be a pity if that were to happen, obscuring two trends in English landownership after 1660. First, though not on anything like the scale, or as universally, as was once believed, estates did get bigger in this period, maintaining a long gradual process that took place from the fifteenth to the nineteenth centuries. Secondly, the century after 1660 was not one of exceptional stability. People continued to cross the gulf into the class of 'gentlemen' as they had done before 1640. In fact, perhaps the most marked feature of the upper reaches of English society in the later seventeenth and early eighteenth centuries is the consolidation and continued slow growth of the wealth and power of a class of landed gentlemen that had increased rapidly in the previous hundred years. In 1873 a survey of land-ownership in Britain revealed that 80 per cent of the land was held by fewer than 7,000 people. Between 1550 and 1750 there took place a significant movement towards that position.

'YEOMEN' AND 'HUSBANDMEN': THE DECLINE OF THE ENGLISH SMALL FARMER

The early modern period was also an important period of social change for those in England who were not wealthy or independent enough to be considered 'gentlemen'. As has been seen, contemporary classifications of such 'middling' rural people as 'yeomen' and 'husbandmen' have been adopted here to describe this social group rather than 'peasantry'. 'Peasant' is too ambiguous a word since it is often used to refer to people who were primarily engaged in subsistence farming and who rarely moved from their small farms [19]. Even at the start of the early modern period England was a market economy and English society was characterised by a high degree of geographical mobility. Many farms were geared to production for the market and few remained in the possession of one family for many generations. Holdings of land in many communities were already unequal. In Kibworth Harcourt in Leicestershire the structure of uniform holdings began to disappear in the thirteenth century and was well advanced by the end of the fourteenth century [57]. In Chippenham in Cambridgeshire in 1544 two farmers held over 100 acres each, twenty-five held between 13 and 83 acres and eighteen had less than 9 acres [67]. The same kind of diversity in farm sizes existed in Myddle in Shropshire, where in the early seventeenth century there were farms ranging from 650 acres to under 10 acres [52]. The terms 'yeomen' for the greater farmers and 'husbandmen' for the smaller farmers were used at the time to describe this diversity in wealth and status that had developed in England by the end of the Middle Ages.

Over two centuries later a marked change had taken place in some English communities. On the eve of the Industrial Revolution, and just after, there were more large and middle-sized farms and fewer small farms than before.

Agricultural England in the nineteenth century presented a unique and amazing spectacle to the inquiring foreigner . . . in practically all the countries from which visitors were at all likely to come to the United Kingdom, the bulk of the people who earned their living by tilling the soil consisted of families owning or occupying their own small plot of land, cultivating it substantially with the labour of their members, and indeed very often – perhaps mostly – still practising subsistence, even when they sold some of their produce in the market, supposing they had a surplus . . . Yet in England they were already unimportant minorities. [244 *p. 3*]

Hobsbawm's and Rude's comment raises important questions for the social historian of early modern England: how extensive was the decline of small farmers and when and why did the social structure of England in this respect diverge from that of much of the rest of Europe?

Historical opinion on these questions during the last hundred years or so has been deeply divided, making apparent that there are no clear straightforward answers to them. Historians have differed both on the timing and explanations of the change. For R. H. Tawney the 'problem' of the disappearance of the bulk of small farmers was a sixteenth-century one, caused largely by the legal insecurity of tenures by which most of them held their farms. The law gave them scant protection against landlords who were intent on raising their rental incomes as a response to the inflation of the period [204]. A. H. Johnson, on the other hand, considered that the later seventeenth and early eighteenth centuries was the most important period and he emphasised falling food prices and high taxes as the crucial factors behind this social change [201]. Other writers have argued that the vital period in the demise of the small farmer was the mid-late eighteenth century, the heyday of parliamentary enclosure, which forced small landowners and tenant farmers alike off the land; while others have sought to show that the decline took place largely after 1815 during the agricultural depression that occurred in the wake of the Napoleonic wars [199]. Confronted by this bewildering array of interpretations the student may be forgiven for feeling very confused. He or she will no doubt feel even worse when confusion is compounded by the fact that some historians emphasise that small farmers persisted as a significant social group in eighteenth- and nineteenth-century England [203]. The phenomenon that some historians seek to explain, these historians seem to suggest, did not in fact take place at all to any great extent!

One starting point for a resolution of this confusion is a realisation that the extent by which small farmers declined in England in the early modern period can be exaggerated. The process of decline clearly was very slow and long. As has been noted, inequality of landholdings had already begun in the Middle Ages and the development of a modern pattern of larger farms and a mass of landless labourers was not completed by the end of the early modern period.

One other point also seems fairly certain and that is that Tawney exaggerated the importance of land tenure as a factor in explaining the fortunes of small farmers, since in the eyes of the common law in the sixteenth and seventeenth centuries many forms of customary tenure were accounted to convey a freehold interest to the occupier. Many prominent early seventeenth-century lawyers, including Sir Edward Coke, declared that any tenure for one life or more technically created a freehold interest [*Doc. 23*]. In these circumstances copyholders holding either by inheritance or for lives had the same legal security of tenure as freeholders. Since this group of tenants probably made up the majority of tenants in early modern England, Tawney's argument becomes highly suspect [202]. It is probable that many small farmers were not as legally vulnerable as was once thought.

What is more, there is a case for believing that small farmers survived and sometimes prospered throughout the early modern period in some parts of England, and especially in those areas identified as 'forest-pasture' regions. Pastoral farms required less labour and capital outlay than arable farms. Moreover, in upland 'forest' areas there were opportunities for farmers to supplement their incomes to carry them through periods of temporary difficulties. Access to waste land as a valuable source of fuel, food and pasture was more common in those areas than in enclosed arable 'champion' areas. Furthermore, as will be pointed out later, commercial manufacturing tended to be concentrated in such areas, giving opportunities for by-employment in cloth-making and other rural industries. What also strengthened the position of small farmers in these regions was that after 1660, when food prices generally fell, it was prices of grain and not of their meat and dairy products that fell dramatically [21]. In addition, these were areas relatively unaffected by enclosures. Brigstock in Rockingham Forest is typical of those woodland villages which had large commons, opportunities both for grazing cattle on the wasteland and for employment in rural manufacturing, and so were able to continue to support a thriving community of small farmers throughout the seventeenth century [63]. The same is true of other forest communities like those in the New Forest in Hampshire and the Forest of Arden district of Warwickshire, as well as pastoral areas like Myddle, the claylands and heaths of west Dorset and the Isle of Purbeck, and the 'cheese' country of Wiltshire [48; 52; 66; 69]. Similarly, the smallholders of the south Lancashire Pennines and Cumbria thrived on a dual economy of farming and textile-weaving and those in the west Midlands and south Yorkshire by combining metal crafts and agriculture [53; 62; 64; 70]. This list is not exhaustive, but indicates the kind of evidence that can be used by those who wish to emphasise continuity in English society in this period.

Clearly, however, changes were taking place: small farmers were being driven out and there was a marked trend towards larger farms in early modern England. This is especially true of 'fielden' communities which were based on sheep-corn economies. Farmers here had few of the opportunities open to those in 'forest-pasture' regions to supplement their farming incomes. In these circumstances the profit margin gained purely from farming was crucial in determining whether or not a farmer could survive. Estimates of the income and expenditure of a small farmer in a 'fielden' area in the early seventeenth century indicate just how precarious life was for such an individual. From his thirty-acre farm he would produce wheat and barley that could be sold for £42 10s 0d (£42.50). Against this, however, has to be set expenditure on seed, rent, manure, feed for oxen and interest and depreciation on equipment and stock, which amounted to £23 15s 9d (£23.79), leaving a net profit for the year of £14 9s 3d (£14.47). Using later estimates of average annual expenditure in order to support a family of six (£11 5s 0d or £11.25), the arable small farmer would be left with £3–5 a year, a small margin that could easily disappear if a harvest failed [159]. Such a position probably faced the small farmers of the arable village of Chippenham in Cambridgeshire, who had all disappeared by 1636, giving way to larger farmers who were in a better position to survive because their working costs were proportionately lower [67].

However, it was probably in the period after 1650 that small arable farmers suffered most. At least before 1650 grain prices continued to rise generally; as has been seen, after 1650 they fell drastically. Small farms with profit margins of £3–£5 a year were often no longer viable and were consequently often amalgamated ('engrossed') into larger farms staffed by a workforce of landless labourers [*Doc. 22*]. This process was especially marked in regions which were most advanced in the adoption of new crops and techniques and in boosting productivity: the sheep-corn areas of East Anglia and the West Country, and the Midland clay vales which were slowly being transformed from arable to pastoral economies. Small farmers were ill-equipped to take part in this economic progress. They had no capital to invest in expensive new techniques like 'floating the water meadows'. The sheep-corn regions of Wiltshire show a marked contrast to the 'cheese' areas. In the former areas family farms declined and the numbers of wage-earning labourers rose from one-third of the population in the early sixteenth century to one-half by the mid-seventeenth century, by which time 'more than half the farmland was occupied by employers of considerable numbers of wage-workers, around over a quarter by gentlemen-farmers and cultivating squires, employing a score or more of wage-workers' [60 *p. 57*]. On the Leveson-Gower estates in Staffordshire and Shropshire in the eighteenth century 'the trend towards larger farms . . . emerges clearly enough' [205 *p. 597*]; and in Moreton Say in Shropshire 'the most important aspect of the agrarian history (of the village) . . . in the eighteenth century was the amalgamation of farms' [59 *p. 24*].

The pattern of continuity and change set out here – continuity in 'forest-pasture' regions and change in 'fielden' areas – is undoubtedly not flexible enough to take account of all kinds of local experiences in rural communities in early modern England. Wigston Magna is a 'fielden' village in which small farmers survived, for example [56]. However, what can be said is that most rural communities do fit into this pattern. In the early modern period in 'fielden' areas everywhere, but especially in counties like Norfolk and Lincolnshire, Hampshire and Wiltshire, in the later seventeenth and early eighteenth centuries, the configurations of a modern pattern of landholding began to emerge, characterised by large farms employing a workforce of wage-earning labourers. Here, if not everywhere, the small independent farmer had disappeared.

LABOURERS, SERVANTS AND VAGRANTS

The number of people reliant on wages for subsistence was growing in early modern England. One wishes that such a generalisation could be demonstrated with the kind of statistics available to historians of British society in the nineteenth and twentieth centuries. Unfortunately, national figures do not exist for this pre-census period but Professor Everitt's estimate of a rise in the wage-earning labouring population of England from about one-quarter of the population in the early sixteenth century to about one-third by the late seventeenth century is the kind of increase seen in many Tudor and Stuart villages [209]. The labouring population of Myddle, for example, grew to 23.4 per cent by 1600 and 31.2 per cent by 1660; in the Essex village of Terling labourers and cottagers made up 27.6 per cent of the population at the time of the 1524–5 subsidy assessment and 50.8 per cent when the Hearth Tax was collected in 1671 [52; 73]. As has been seen in the last section, there was a marked trend, especially in 'fielden' areas, towards large farms employing wage-earning labourers. To these must be added the growing numbers of those who worked as domestic servants, employed by wealthy landowners, farmers and by the expanding and increasingly prosperous classes of manufacturers, merchants and professional people. Taken together, labourers and servants made up the biggest section of early modern English society.

They were also the most vulnerable of all social groups to the impact of economic change. The fifteenth century, with its stagnant population and prices, might have been 'the golden age of the English labourer' (as Thorold Rogers described it) [169], but when population and price trends began to move upwards at the end of the century that golden age undoubtedly came to an end. Typical daily wage rates of agricultural labourers rose from 4d (2p) to 12d (5p) and those of building craftsmen from 6d (2p) to 1s 5d (7p) between 1500 and 1640, but these did not match the rise in prices.

At their lowest point in this pre-1640 period, the second decade of the seventeenth century, real daily wage rates of farm labourers had fallen to 44 per cent and those of building craftsmen to 39 per cent, of the level they had been during the last half of the fifteenth century. These calculations, of course, ignore regional variations in wage rates, which were probably higher in London and south-eastern counties than elsewhere (although there is a dearth of material on this aspect of social history). But they suggest something of the plight of the wage-earner in this period, especially when periodic runs of bad harvests or crises in the woollen cloth trade probably hit them very hard. The 1620s, 1630s and 1640s 'witnessed extreme hardship in England, and were probably among the most terrible years through which the country has ever passed. It was probably no coincidence that the first real beginnings in the colonization of America date from this period' [159 *p. 621*].

It is also for this reason that the labourers and servants of early modern society were often forced to take to the roads of England in search of work. It would be wrong to discount altogether the con-temporary descriptions of such wandering people as shiftless and idle, roaming the countryside often in bands, a threat to respectable society [*Doc. 31*]. But there seems little doubt that the majority of poor migrants, whether moving short or long distances, from 'fielden' to forest areas or from countryside to town, took to the roads out of economic necessity. Also, in contrast to the view of writers of hysterical tracts, most migrants as they appear in the records (e.g. proceedings against over 1,100 vagrants arrested in eighteen counties in the Elizabethan period, and passports given to vagrants by the town authorities of Salisbury between 1598 and 1638 and Colchester between 1630 and 1640) seem to have been men and women, often in their late teens and early twenties and travelling alone [206–7; 212] [*Doc. 26*]. Bands of 'sturdy beggars' threatening property and lives were much rarer than a reading of sixteenth- and early seventeenth-century official pronouncements and treatises might indicate. But many labourers and servants were forced by economic need to travel the highways and byways of Elizabethan and early Stuart England. Moreover, as has been noted already, poverty remained a fact of life for a mass of people in the later part of the early modern period. Gregory King's class of 'labourers, cottagers and paupers' who were 'decreasing the wealth of the kingdom' consisted of 2,575,000 people in 1688, i.e. 46 per cent of the total population as calculated by the Cambridge Group. Even the sternest critics of King's statistics do not deny that they indicate a continuing bedrock of poverty in early modern England.

Yet life for all wage-earning labourers and servants was not deteriorating, even in the harsh climate of the inflationary sixteenth and early seventeenth centuries, and in the century after 1650 conditions improved markedly in their favour. Although the conditions of life of all labourers and servants were broadly similar, there were crucial differences between them. One of the most important is that between two different types of farm labourers. The first were often called 'servants in husbandry', who were hired on annual contracts and often lived and ate with the farmer and his family. Most of these were young adults under twenty-five years of age and unmarried. When their contracts expired most of them moved to new masters [210]. Clearly the life-styles of 'servants in husbandry' were different from, and their fortunes more secure than, those of agricultural wage-labourers, who spent all their lives in that occupation, were paid by the day and had no guarantee of constant employment. Indeed, seasonal unemployment affected this group greatly. Yet even among day labourers there were great variations in conditions of life, largely depending on whether they had means of supplementing their wages by living and eating in the houses of their employers, by growing food on a smallholding, by securing part-time jobs in rural industries or by benefiting from wages earned by their wives and children, who were commonly employed in agricultural work. It may be that, as in the case of small farmers, these opportunities for supplementing subsistence were more available in wood-pasture areas than elsewhere, which accounts for the tendency of these regions to be magnets of rural migration. It may be, too, that poor-relief systems at least limited the worst effects of poverty in Tudor and early Stuart England and prevented labourers and servants from suffering from the full impact of the Price Revolution in the sixteenth and early seventeenth centuries.

With the end of the Price Revolution came a century of stagnating or falling food prices. What made this situation especially advantageous to wage-earners was that it was accompanied by a declining population; labour was in short supply and so, in money terms, wage rates were likely to rise. A recent estimate indicates that the real wage rates of building craftsmen (on a base of 100 for the decade 1680–9) rose from 96 in 1650–9 to 110 in 1700–9 and 129 in 1740–9 [33]. Agricultural wage rates rose less steeply, by 5 per cent in money terms and 12 per cent in real terms between 1640 and 1749 [160]. As yet there are only a few local examples to support this point, though an early eighteenth-century

Nottinghamshire day-labourer probably needed a gross income of £8–£9 a year to buy food, clothes, fuel and tools and pay rent. This could be earned by an average wage of 8d (3p) a day for 300 days in the year and still leave a surplus of £1. In reality basic agricultural wage rates were higher than 8d a day in that period and many male labourers' wages would be supplemented from other sources, like wages earned by wives and children [49; 165]. Obviously one has to be sceptical of contemporary pamphleteers who claimed that early eighteenth-century labourers could earn enough to live on in three or four days a week, but their comments are in line with scattered evidence of rising real wage rates (both of females and males) in the later seventeenth and early eighteenth centuries in a wide range of counties in southern England with both pastoral and arable economies [213] [*Doc. 25*]. This coincided with a period from 1730 to 1750 of exceptionally low food prices, the result of a succession of good harvests and rising agricultural productivity [39]. It is perhaps pushing the evidence too far to suggest that the century after 1650 was a second golden age for the English labourer but, as D. C. Coleman writes, 'despite short-term reversals, for example in the 1690s and 1709–12, there was probably a moderate, long- term increase in disposable income for many wage-earners' [33 *p. 103*].

CRAFTSMEN AND TRADESMEN

In every English town and village in this period there were, of course, men and women who produced consumer goods for the local urban and rural population, making and selling food and drink (e.g. butchers, bakers, brewers), clothing (e.g. cappers, tanners, shoemakers), furniture, household and farm implements, and tools (e.g. carpenters, coopers and blacksmiths). It is not surprising that some contemporaries, as has been noted, were uncertain where to place such people in the social hierarchy, because, although some were engaged in these occupations full-time, most were also farmers and farm workers. Much manufacturing of all kinds – whether for local or national and international markets – was done by people who also worked on the land. This has caused some historians to write about the existence of a 'dual economy'.

The regional variations in the pattern of the dual economy match the variety of goods that were produced [32]. The principal manufactured product in early modern England was woollen cloth. In areas of the West Country, where its manufacture was highly geared to the national and international market, many workers spent more time on spinning and weaving than they did on farming. Indeed in the forested areas along the border of east Somerset and western Wiltshire there emerged a class of artisans who were almost totally dependent on the industry for their living. On the other hand, in the West Riding of Yorkshire woollen cloth production was a much more peripheral activity for farmers. There were also variations in the degree of dependence of rural manufacturers on merchant-entrepreneurs for supplies of raw materials and for selling the finished product. In the highly commercialised sectors of the woollen cloth industry, including parts of East Anglia [*Doc. 28*] as well as the West Country, farmer-spinners and weavers were part of a complex operation controlled by wealthier clothiers, like the Tuckers of Burford and Springs of Lavenham in the sixteenth century and Benedict Webb in the West Country in the early seventeenth century, who bought the wool and who sometimes owned the looms that were hired out to rural workers; while in the West Riding woollen cloth (though not worsteds, when the pro-duction of these developed in the eighteenth century) was produced mainly by farmers who grew their own wool, which was spun and woven by themselves and their families and then sold at local cloth markets.

There were many other consumer goods produced in early modern England besides woollen cloth. Until recently, however, they have received little attention from historians. This neglect is now being rectified and there are good studies of other important manufactures: for example, the leather industry [31], which produced goods from saddles to gloves and shoes, the frame-work-knitting hosiery industry, and the metal industries, which produced a variety of implements like nails and scythes [64]. These industries had the same diversity of organisation as the woollen cloth industry. The metal industries had great ironmasters, but more typical were smaller ironmongers in the west Midlands, who bought and distributed bar iron to nailers and scythemen who worked as handicraftsmen in their own homes. Joan Thirsk's Ford Lectures have done most to reveal the diversity of the manufacturing economy of early modern England [288]. She shows how many people were engaged in (among many other things) button-making, the production of pins and nails, salt, starch, soap, knives and tools, tobacco pipes, pots and ovens, ribbon and lacemaking, linen-weaving, and the cultivation of vegetable dyes. The growing and manufacture of woad, for example, she reckons provided employment for 2,000 people in twelve southern counties in 1586.

But whatever the scale, the essential features of the organisation of these industries remained the same. The manufacturing work was done largely in villages or hamlets in the houses of farmers and farm workers; it was labour-intensive, most of the capital involved was invested in raw materials and not in fixed capital (plant or machinery); and sometimes the organisation was directed by a merchant-entrepreneur. This domestic system of manufacturing prevailed throughout the early modern period, which is a fact that requires some explanation, given its obvious disadvantages from an economic point of view. Not only were the distribution costs of putting-out and collecting materials high, but there were few constraints on pilfering and (most serious of all) the lack of supervision of the kind that exists in a factory made it very difficult to maintain uniform standards of quality in finished products. That the domestic system persisted despite these considerations is accounted for by the fact that it was well suited to the nature of pre-industrialised society. Irregular, fluctuating demand for manufactured goods did not encourage those with money to invest it and tie it up in plant and factories. It was much more convenient, cheaper and easier to use rural labour and lay it off when demand slackened. Indeed the prime advantage of the system was that it tapped the pool of underemployed rural labour that was available in early modern England [208].

Even in 1800 only the spinning side of the cotton industry had changed over to the factory system; even the few capital-intensive enterprises such as iron-smelting, mining, milling and shipbuilding were done on a small scale; and most manufacturing was done as handcraft. This essential continuity, however, ought not to obscure the fact that changes did take place in English manufacturing in the early modern period, which had a major impact on the structure of English society. The concentration of manufacturing in certain regions was not new, but it did undoubtedly accelerate in this period. This was first established by Joan Thirsk, who pointed to the concentration of manufacturing in forest-pasture regions of England [42]. There, underemployment was much more common than in sheep–corn areas with their labour-intensive economies; pastoral agriculture like dairying and stock-keeping allowed families more time for by-employments. In these areas, too, where population densities were often high, holdings were smaller and partible inheritance more common than in sheep–corn regions, families often relied on by-employments for subsistence. Dr Thirsk never claimed that this was the only explanation of the location of manufacturing. There were many others, like availability of raw materials and access to water power. The absence of a resident lord was a key factor in the growth of framework knitting in the Leicestershire villages of Shepshed and Wigston Magna; in the latter by 1700 one-sixth of households were largely dependent on it [56; 90]. Nor was all manufacturing done in the countryside. Centralised enterprises like shipbuilding and soap-boiling were located in towns, as were sections of the woollen cloth industry. Between 1540 and 1590 42 per cent of the population of Worcester was engaged in cloth-making on domestic lines, for example.

Yet it is remarkable how frequently local studies show a growing density of populations engaged in manufacturing in upland areas with a mixed pastoral farming economy. This is true of most of the major industrial areas of early modern England. At least three of the four major woollen textile regions (the West Country, Devon and Somerset, and the West Riding of Yorkshire), as well as lesser ones like Kendal in Westmorland, fall into this category. So too do other textile-producing regions: linen and fustian production in south Lancashire and framework knitting in parts of Nottinghamshire and Leicestershire, for example. It is true also of the west Midlands' small metalware industries and cutlery-making in south Yorkshire [53; 64]. The relationship becomes even clearer when detailed work is done on these areas. South Staffordshire followed largely a wood–pasture economy with livestock-rearing. Here, ample waste and grazing attracted landless squatters, who joined a labour force engaged in raising cattle and making nails, locks and spurs. These handicraftsmen were supplied with bar iron by middlemen from Birmingham, Wolverhampton and Dudley. But in nearby areas of the county with better soils, there developed a mixed farming economy which attracted few immigrants and consequently rural industry did not develop there to any great extent [51]. Similarly, on the chalklands of Dorset only spinning developed alongside a predominantly sheep–corn husbandry. However, on the claylands and heath areas of west Dorset and the Isle of Purbeck where stock-rearing was the main agrarian occupation, a variety of industries was carried on: hemp-growing for making rope, twine and fishing nets, and leather crafts (saddles, boots and gloves); while in the woodlands of north and west Dorset local farmers made hurdles and rakes [48].

As the period progressed some people in these areas became more and more dependent on manufacturing for a living. For example, in the wood-pasture communities of south Staffordshire the proportion of metal workers who owned cattle, pigs and sheep dropped steadily in the seventeenth century: from an average of 60.5 per cent in 1600 to 37.6 per cent in the period between 1681 and 1721. For many, 'a vista of increasing dependence on cash income from forge products was opened up' [51 p. 41]. This was especially true of west Midland nailers in the Walsall, Dudley, Wolverhampton, and Stourbridge areas (though not of scythemakers who continued to combine their work with farming for much longer), the cutlers and nailmakers of the south Yorkshire villages around Sheffield, pottery workers in north Staffordshire, cloth workers in the Stroud region of Gloucestershire, hosiery framework knitters in Leicestershire and Nottinghamshire [*Doc. 27*], and those occupied in distilling, sugar refining, glass-making and brassworking around Bristol. In few communities that have been studied did this process go as far as Kibworth Harcourt in Leicestershire, where the farmer-craftsman had disappeared altogether by 1700 [57]. But in some areas there had been a marked trend away from the dual economy. In 1750 there were more rural workers in domestic industry, as well as specialist craftsmen and tradesmen in towns who were primarily dependent on manufacturing for a living, than there had been in 1550, thus adding to the increasing plurality and complexity of English society by the end of the early modern period.

MERCHANTS AND PROFESSIONAL PEOPLE: THE GROWTH OF 'THE MONIED INTEREST'

To contemporaries, the abundance of craftsmen and tradesmen was not the most noticeable (and to some, worrying) manifestation of the growing importance in English society of people whose wealth did not come directly from land. This is the growth of what some began to label 'the monied interest': wealthy manufacturers, merchants and financiers, and those whom we now call 'professional' people. These groups were all, of course, present in English society at the end of the Middle Ages, but between 1550 and 1750 there was a remarkable growth in their numbers, wealth and status.

Of these groups, manufacturers were fewer in number and less important. Given the predominance of the domestic system of manufacturing the age of the major industrialist was in the future. Yet there were a few entrepreneurs in the late seventeenth and early eighteenth centuries who operated large-scale commercial organisations, like the Foley brothers, Paul and Philip, who were among a small group of ironmasters in the west Midlands. By 1700 the Foleys owned forty iron mills in the west Midlands, the Forest of Dean and South Wales and their business had a capital of £39,000 subscribed by five shareholders. Even wealthier was a north-eastern ironmaster, Sir Ambrose Crowley, who began producing nails in Durham in 1684 and then built slitting mills, furnaces and forges at Winlaton near Newcastle, from which he supplied the navy with chains and anchors. He soon had a mini-industrial empire, buying bar iron from other ironmasters in the Midlands and in Sweden, and owning a fleet of ships that sailed between the north east and London. By 1728 his estate was valued at £250,000 [46; 64]. Outside the iron industry there were few such giants, although some brewers operated on a large scale, like Ben Truman whose business was valued at £23,000 in 1740.

More numerous were wealthy merchants, a direct result of 'the commercial revolution' of the seventeenth century. This is one of the few unchallenged 'revolutions' of the early modern period [34]. The contrasts between English overseas trade in 1550 and in 1750 are stark. In 1550 England's foreign trade was directed largely to northern Europe, exporting traditional woollen broadcloths (undyed and unfinished); this was the eve of the first of a series of major crises from which trade suffered during the next century, when native merchants had to compete with foreign merchants in the handling of English trade. By 1750, in contrast, English trade had broken out of this strait-jacket; trade was directed to southern as well as to northern Europe, Africa, the Far East India and China – and across the Atlantic to the new English colonies in America and the Caribbean. The goods traded in were equally diverse: re-exports of goods like sugar, tobacco and Indian textiles, and many kinds of English manufactured goods other than woollen cloth. Provincial ports like Liverpool, Bristol, Hull and (after the Act of Union in 1707) Glasgow had grown enormously and now challenged the predominance of London in overseas trade. Moreover, trade was now not only more broadly based, it was prosperous, expanding and largely in the hands of native merchants. There have, however, been fewer studies of these merchants and their fortunes than of landowners, principally because few merchants' archives survive. Yet studies of those merchants about whom records do exist, either because they later became landowners, like Sir John Banks, Governor of the East India Company, or because they already were landowners, like the Lowthers of Whitehaven, who developed large-scale interests in the coal and tobacco trades to and from Whitehaven, suggest that large amounts of wealth were accumulated by a few [170-1].

Seventeenth-century London provides the most systematic evidence of this. Few London merchants were as rich as Lionel Cranfield (later earl of Middlesex), or Sir John Spencer in the reign of James I who reputedly owned goods valued at £400,000 when he died. But of the 140 aldermen of Jacobean London 55 were worth over £20,000 a year and many of the remaining 85 left personal estates (excluding landed wealth) of between £10,000 and £20,000 [226]. At the end of the seventeenth century the wealth of the capital's mercantile community was even more impressive [220]. Moreover, it was not only merchants trading overseas who became wealthy. Over half of the merchants of Jacobean London, for example, made their fortunes in the domestic distributive trades. By the next century this pattern was repeated in many other towns. 'Greater merchants and wholesale dealers were often prominent among the social elites of eighteenth-century towns' [26 *p. 131*].

The growing wealth of the country on which mercantile prosperity was based fuelled a parallel social change: the rising importance of professional people, another branch of the social elite whose wealth and power was not exclusively based on land [229]. As usual in this period, national statistics to illustrate this are non-existent. Yet many local studies underline the fact that this was a social change that was already underway in the sixteenth and early seventeenth centuries. In Norwich the number of doctors trebled between 1525 and 1575 [274]. In Northampton the percentage of the town's wealth held by professional people grew from 'virtually nil' in 1611 to 10 per cent by 1640 [15]. Some indication of the proliferation of lawyers in early modern society is given by the fact that between 1500 and 1639, 2,767 were called to the bar, of whom the bulk (2,138) were called in the last fifty years of the period [228]. J. H. Raach's directory of early seventeenth-century physicians, which undoubtedly includes only a fraction of the total, has 814 outside London, with seventeen in Norwich, twenty-two in Canterbury, thirteen in Exeter and ten in York [231]. At the same time there were significant developments *within* the major professions, reflecting their enhanced status.

This generalisation needs to be qualified regarding the Church. Its economic problems outlined by Christopher Hill, in what has a claim to be his best book, remained largely unsolved in the early modern period [221]. Most of the major tithes, which had originally been part of the endowments of churches to provide the main source of clerical incomes, were now impropriated by secular land-owners as part of their rental incomes. Every major effort in the early modern period to recover them for the Church failed to overcome the obstacle of propertied vested interest. Salaries of ordinary parochial clergymen generally, therefore, remained low throughout the period and it was not uncommon for Tudor and Stuart vicars to supplement their incomes by farming. Most of the sixteenth-century Lincolnshire clergymen who left probate inventories had farming implements among their possessions [218]. Ralph Josselin, the mid seventeenth-century vicar of Earls Colne in Essex, was a farmer as well as village parson [92]. In Leicestershire the gross incomes of seventeenth-century clergymen may have risen in the later part of the century, though it is likely that much of the increase was wiped out by heavy taxation, especially during the war years at the end of the century [230]. Yet despite all this, in the century before 1650 the ecclesiastical profession began to attract better-educated young men. In 1551 over half of the church ministers in the diocese of Gloucester were said to be so ignorant that they were unable to repeat the Ten Commandments. A century later most clergymen were university graduates [227].

Developments within the legal and medical professions reflect a similar growth of professional self-esteem, as barristers attempted to establish their elite position as practitioners in the central law courts by distancing themselves from attorneys, who were only to represent litigants in court, and solicitors, who were only to act as clients' representatives in legal transactions outside courts. The medical elite, the physicians, also attempted to prevent apothecaries from diagnosing illnesses and from prescribing drugs as well as supplying them. The development of an internal hierarchy within the medical profession is marked by the establishment of the Royal College of Physicians in 1518, the College of Barber Surgeons in 1540 and the Society of Apothecaries in 1617. In reality, attempts to establish restrictive practices were not totally successful. The typical late sixteenth- or early seventeenth-century doctor or lawyer was a general practitioner. But the growing volume of hostility to professional groups in the literature of the period (and especially in the 1640s and 1650s) [222] is an indication of the growing prominence of those who provided professional services in Tudor and early Stuart England.

It was the century after 1650, however, that witnessed a significant acceleration in both the numbers and status of clerics, lawyers [*Doc. 29*] and doctors. There also took place 'the slow crystallisation of a number of new vocational groups, which began to take on an embryonic professional identity' [*225 p. 21*]. For example, there was a possible increase of 2,000 schoolteachers between 1680 and 1730 and, although not yet a fully fledged profession, schoolteaching was 'more generally regarded as a true vocation in 1730 than in 1680' [*225 p. 80*]. Similarly, the prosperity of great landowners during the same period led to the appearance of a rash of people providing services to meet their needs: architects, landscape gardeners, surveyors, land agents and estate stewards.

At the same time there was an expansion in the number of civil servants. Before the mid-seventeenth century the bureaucracy of the English state was tiny. One of the major political–constitutional developments of later Stuart–early Hanoverian England is a growth in the size of central government departments, accounted for largely by the pressures of war and changes in attitudes. The latter – the growth of 'political arithmetic' – will be discussed later (see Chapter 12). It coincided with a period when warfare had a greater impact on English society than ever before. The Civil War (1642–52) and the European wars of 1689–1713, 1739–48 and 1756–63 did not have the same effect on society as the two World Wars of this century; but their scale and expense (especially the wars after 1689) brought about an expansion of the royal bureaucracy that marked a decisive change from the medieval structure of English central government. The process is seen earliest and most clearly in the Treasury, which came to rival the Exchequer as the main institution of public finance [232]. Given the enormous demands of men, money and supplies to fight late seventeenth- and early eighteenth-century wars, it is not surprising that it was the financial, military, naval and diplomatic departments that expanded most dramatically, staffed by civil servants like Samuel Pepys (Secretary to the Admiralty 1673–9 and 1684–8) and William Blathwayt (Secretary at War from 1683 under four successive monarchs). By 1759 Joseph Massie reckoned that Gregory King's group of 10,000 civil servants had swollen to 16,000. A greater contrast is, however, with the 1,000 or so people that staffed the civil service of Charles I [214].

An allied social change brought about by warfare after 1689 was the growing importance of those who invested in government stock. A meticulously detailed analysis of those who lent money to the government of William III, desperate for means to fight the war against France in the early 1690s, reveals a group that became a permanent part of the social scene in the eighteenth century. Just over half of the 5,000 people who lent money by subscribing to the Tontine of 1693 and the Bank of England in 1694 are known. Of these a few were landowners; some were of recent French Huguenot descent (53 lent to the Tontine and 123 to the Bank); fewer still were Jews (six lent money in 1693 and four in 1694); but 'the majority of subscribers to both loans belong to the mercantile middle classes of London, though there were also important ancillary contributions from lawyers, office-holders, and the clergy of the Church of England' [219 *p. 265*]. Between 1689 and 1756 'war and war finance had brought into a position of very considerable power a group of capitalists of international outlook and connections and of mixed origins . . . Nearly all were self-made men, whose wealth had been built up during the long wars since 1689' [219 *pp. 297–8*].

Between 1694 and 1713 the expansion of some of these new non-landed social elites in England became an issue of major political controversy. As the war against France was prolonged the early enthusiasm felt by many landed gentlemen for it evaporated. A sequence of allied victories and heavy war taxation seemed to have brought an end to the war no nearer. This fact spawned a stream of complaints that the war was being prolonged in order to line the pockets of the 'monied interest' – dissenters and foreigners, Huguenots, Dutchmen and Jews – who were profiting from the interest on loans made to the Crown. This is why Dr Sacheverell received so much militant support when he delivered explosive sermons in the early 1700s voicing fears that the traditional society and the Church were being challenged by 'the monied interest'. The political propaganda of the period came, in fact, to depict England as a 'divided society', 'the monied interest' versus 'the landed interest' [223–4] [*Doc. 30*]. Like most political propaganda the literature of the early 1700s distorts historical reality. Social divisions were not as clear-cut as they were said to be. Landowners invested in the Bank of England and in government stock, as they did in trading companies. Their antipathy to 'the monied interest' did not prevent them from marrying into it or from allowing their sons to join the world of finance, trade and the professions. Nor did 'the monied interest' grow on a scale that justified the hysterical outbursts of the period. Even the biggest estimates of the number of non-landed elites considered in this section are tiny in comparison with those within traditional landed society in England.

Yet such outbursts ought not to be disregarded completely. That there were tensions between landed gentlemen and the new 'pseudo' gentlemen of 'the monied interest' suggests that the latter were not easily assimilated into traditional society and that they became an important non-landed element within the social structure of England during the early modern period.

Did, then, this period see the emergence of a new social group, 'the rise of the middling sort'? Some social historians suggest that it did [10]. Others are even willing to go further and write about the existence of 'the middle class' in eighteenth-century England [5]. One obvious danger in using such terminology is that it might obscure the extraordinary diversity of wealth, status and beliefs of the middling groups in English society that have been identified in the last two sub-sections of this chapter. The difference in lifestyles and attitudes between (say) a great merchant-maufacturer like Sir Ambrose Crowley and a small independent craftsman in London casts doubt on making too much of the group cohesion (or 'class consciousness') of 'the middling sort' [12]. Yet, it is true that terms like 'the middling sort' are not without their uses for social historians of early modern England. They facilitate more sophisticated social analyses than do models which are based on sharp distinctions between 'elite' and 'popular' (or 'patrician' and 'plebeian') society. With all its drawbacks 'the middling sort' label at least enables social historians to reflect the growing significance in later seventeenth- and early eighteenth-century England of social groups who do not fit into the traditional landed hierarchy of 'ranks' and 'orders'. Their growing importance also underlines the fact that in this case, as well as in others, the late seventeenth and early eighteenth centuries were years of rapid social change in great contrast to the traditional view of them as a period which saw 'an increasingly immobile society'. During the century after 1650 the pace of social change quickened, producing a social framework that had grown greatly in complexity and diversity since 1550.

8 POVERTY AND DEARTH

It is easier to explain the prevalence of poverty in early modern English society than it is to assess the size of the poverty problem. Most of the statistics on poverty in this period are drawn from urban sources and therefore may not reflect accurately the scale of rural poverty. There is also a possibility that contemporary attempts to calculate the scale of poverty from the mid-sixteenth century onwards may reflect a new awareness of the problems posed by poverty rather than an increase in its incidence, which casts doubts on commonly held views that poverty was increasing rapidly in the sixteenth and seventeenth centuries. These doubts are supported by evidence both of increasing agricultural productivity, which enabled England before 1650 to escape from the kind of subsistence crises which afflicted other parts of Europe, and of a growing demand in England for consumer goods. The implication of this and other evidence regarding general standards of living in early modern England will be examined in the next section.

Such new perspectives, however, ought not to obscure the fact that poverty was a predominant feature of early modern English society. Indeed preceding sections have emphasised that this was so and have pointed to major explanations of it. Vigorously though the sixteenth- and early seventeenth-century economy responded to the challenge, it was unable to absorb fully a growing population. Underemployment was common, labour was cheap and real wage rates fell. Consequently, all labourers, but especially those in areas where industry was becoming concentrated, in towns and 'wood-pasture' regions, were likely to become poorer. Even after 1650 when real wage rates picked up, those labourers who were becoming increasingly dependent on wages from manufacturing were vulnerable to the effects of short-term trade crises when wage rates plummeted temporarily or they were laid off. Small farmers too found life increasingly difficult in the early modern period, especially those in arable, 'fielden' areas, and their fortunes suffered when the harvest failed or (after 1650) when grain prices underwent a long-term slump. There can be little doubt that in the century after 1550 a greater proportion of the population than in the previous 150 years lived on or very near the basic subsistence level. In the century after 1650, as the demographic pressure on resources eased, the situation of many poor people must have become less precarious. But, as has been seen before, poverty remained a central feature of English society.

Some of the symptoms of this situation have also been seen already, most notably vagrancy and the high incidence of geographical mobility generally. The history of crime and of riots and popular disturbances also gives some support to this picture of widespread poverty. Indicted offences (and especially indicted offences against property) rose in many English counties in years of economic crisis, like the 1590s and 1620s and early 1630s. Moreover, the connection between economic conditions and crime is demonstrated in Essex, where not only did the crisis years of the 1620s see the highest level of serious crime recorded in the seventeenth century but it was the textile-producing regions of north-east Essex that were especially prone to sharp increases in crime. The woollen cloth workers there were more dependent on wages for their income than were other rural poor and therefore were less cushioned against the effects of high food prices [255–6]. It is not difficult to see why poor people resorted to theft as a means of supplementing their income in these circumstances. Clearly also some of the riots and popular disturbances of this period were a reaction to economic distress. Rioting as a form of social protest has a long history in England and the early modern period is peppered with it, most notably riots caused by the scarcity of food and high food prices, and disorders provoked by enclosures. Food riots, particularly, were common in years when the harvest failed and grain prices were high [242–52].

Patterns of crime and of riots undoubtedly provide confirmation of the widespread existence of economic hardship in early modern England. However, they also sound a warning note about the nature of the reaction of the poor to their harsh life-styles. What they show is that the poor of early modern England were rarely pushed by poverty into extreme and violent protest. Between the early seventeenth and early eighteenth centuries the number of serious criminal felonies, especially property offences, actually fell [254]. Moreover, after 1549 there was no large-scale popular rebellion in early modern England. In contrast to the view of members of the governing class, who saw riots as the harbingers of revolution by 'the many-headed monster' [*Doc. 31*], popular disturbances were usually remarkably ordered and legalistic in form and conservative in their demands. Rioters demanded not that the social–political world should be turned upside-down or that the law be overturned but that existing laws should be put into effect. It is doubtful whether even during the English Revolution riots diverged from this conservative pattern [250]. Certainly the Levellers appealed only to a restricted section of 'the middling sort' in London and their programme contained little that was likely to have gained the support of the mass of rural poor.

Given the undoubted existence of widespread poverty, the diminishing rate of crime against poverty and the lack of any widely based popular rebellion in early modern England need some explanation. Students looking for a clear answer to this historical puzzle from social historians will be disappointed. It is one of the many aspects of early modern English social history that still requires adequate explanation.

The best starting-point for investigating this puzzle is the work of E. P. Thompson on food riots in eighteenth-century England. In it he explained that rioters at that time shared with the authorities a belief that there was a 'just' price for food and that there were customary regulations forbidding merchants from taking grain away from stricken areas in times of poor harvests. This idea he called 'the moral economy', which, he argued convincingly, drove rioters to protest not in order to overturn the existing social and political order, but to ensure that the law was upheld [249]. Features of English society that have already been noted may also account for the absence of the kind of violent, large-scale popular rebellions that occurred in contemporary France. The poor may have been insulated from the worst effects of harvest failure and poverty by the support offered by strong bonds of neighbourliness noted in Chapter 6. This was part of a complex network of informal poor relief that J. Walter has called 'a social economy' [252]. Migration, noted in Chapter 2, may also have acted as a safety valve which prevented harsh economic conditions from breeding rebellion. Ironically, migration, which was seen by the respectable as a threat to the existing social order, may have helped to maintain it by defusing social tensions that might have built up in closed village communities. Community festivities and amusements, too, may have served a similar function, by imposing a sense of communal unity on both rich and poor. It is also possible that some festivities included elements of role-reversal, which by allowing the normal order of society to be overturned for one day strengthened that order for the rest of the year [121]. The role of the Church may also have been important in this respect, since its teaching reinforced the ordered 'world view' of society seen earlier. The argument that rebellion was a sin, and also that poverty was a punishment for sins committed and therefore had to be borne, was a powerful one that may have gained acceptance by being constantly repeated in sermons [252].

Among many other features of early modern England that may account for the lack of serious social disorder is the emergence in the later sixteenth century of an official system of poor relief that may have mitigated the worst effects of poverty. It may also have helped to tighten the bonds of patronage between rich and poor and therefore to keep the poor well away from the brink of rebellion. This is, of course, a far cry from the way that the Tudor and Stuart poor law has often been interpreted. R. H. Tawney saw it as a cruel and heartless system, while W. K. Jordan in an influential study argued that private charity increased greatly in this period and was much more significant in the relief of poverty than the statutory poor law [204; 237]. Both views are open to question. The statutory poor law had some success in relieving poverty [239], and Jordan overstated the monetary value of private charitable contributions by failing to take into account the fall in the value of money in the sixteenth and early seventeenth centuries. It is true that Jordan's conclusions have been partially rehabilitated by evidence that private charity did at least keep in line with inflation, but it is significant that private philanthropy represents only between 0.25 and 0.5 per cent of current national income in any decade between 1480 and 1660 [235–6].

It is now clear that private charity needs to be seen merely as one part of a remarkable reaction to the problem of poverty by a wide range of people in authority, and not simply by Puritans who had no monopoly of interest in, and concern for, the poor [*Doc. 32*]. Urban authorities were the first to react to the problem, largely because they were affected by it most seriously as poor migrants swarmed into many towns. Their response, by founding hospitals (in London), levying compulsory poor rates and building workhouses (in the later sixteenth and early seventeenth centuries and again from the 1690s) is well-known. Less well-known is the response of the Crown and privy council to the poverty problem by pro-clamations controlling grain prices and supplies and especially by the practice of issuing Books of Orders to local authorities, listing measures for the relief of poverty [239]. Many of these measures evolved by local authorities and by the Crown were then enacted by parliament in the famous statutes of 1572, 1597, 1603 and 1662, which recognised that not all poor people were poor by choice, that only the 'sturdy' poor should be punished and that the 'impotent' poor needed help, and that relief should be provided by rates levied on the inhabitants of the parishes where paupers were born. Taken together, private charity, municipal schemes, government orders and parliamentary statutes are a remarkable response to the early modern poverty problem.

The key historical question about this response, however, is how effectively did it relieve poverty? It is now fairly certain that during the course of the seventeenth century the poor-law system was gradually put into operation in all parishes. Moreover, when the central government put the full weight of its pressure behind the system, as in the 1630s and 1650s, it worked well. In addition, not only were poor rates regularly levied but the total collected increased. In c. 1650 about £250,000 was raised in compulsory poor rates; by 1700 this had risen to £700,000 [240]. The material benefits in money, food and fuel, often given in the form of outdoor relief, however, may not have been the sole (or main) contribution of the poor law in maintaining social order. The poor law also had a social as well as a monetary value: it was an affirmation of the patronage system, which it has been seen held early modern English society together. The generosity to the poor of those in authority was not simply an altruistic gesture; it was made out of a recognition that 'the poor had to be continually won over. Charity was extracted as well as bestowed, poor relief demanded as well as administered' [251 *p. 142*]. In towns like late seventeenth-century Newcastle 'the authorities had a healthy respect for the limits of their effective jurisdiction', which accounts for poor relief schemes in the town and for the way that 'employers dealt with grievances with a practical conciliatory attitude' [263 *p. 216*]. The poor responded with obedience and deference, but this had been gained at a price.

In all these ways before 1650 it is likely that the social tensions arising out of poverty were contained. After 1650 these tensions eased. The effect of a century of slow population growth not only made the condition of life of the poor less precarious but it also caused the poor to be seen by the governing classes as less of a threat to the social order [*Doc. 33*]. This is certainly one explanation for the remarkable discovery that 'despite the increase of capital statutes from the late seventeenth century onwards executions fell'; in the later seventeenth century only about one-tenth of the number of convicted criminals were being executed compared with one hundred years previously [256 *p. 182*]. There seems little doubt that this (as well as the decline in indicted property offences) is a symptom of the more relaxed relations between rich and poor that were possible in the new economic context of the period between 1650 and 1750.

9   AFFLUENCE AND PROSPERITY

THE EMERGENCE OF AN URBAN SOCIETY

Neither in 1550 nor in 1750 could England be described as an urbanised society. Even at the end of the period over three-quarters of the population still lived in the countryside. Yet the early modern period did see a remarkable growth of the urban sector in English society [261–2]. In 1550 there was only one large town, London, with a population of between 60,000 and 80,000 inhabitants, which overshadowed even the largest of provincial towns. Only two of them, Norwich and Bristol, had reached the 10,000 mark and there are only five other towns (York, Exeter, Newcastle, Salisbury and Oxford) which one can be fairly certain had over 5,000 inhabitants. Even fifty years later only about 8 per cent of the country's population lived in towns of over 5,000 inhabitants and only 3 per cent lived in such towns outside London. By 1750 a marked change had taken place. London's population had risen to 675,000 inhabitants and still far outstripped in size the leading provincial towns. Yet the population of provincial towns was growing at a faster rate than that of the capital and there were now nineteen provincial towns with populations of over 10,000 inhabitants and another thirty-one with between 5,000 and 10,000 inhabitants. By now, 19.9 per cent of the population lived in towns of 5,000 inhabitants and over. Moreover, whereas in the sixteenth and early seventeenth centuries the urban population had grown only at the same rate as the national population, during the century after 1650 the urban population grew at a faster rate than the population of the country as a whole. Clearly the early modern period (and especially the later seventeenth and early eighteenth centuries) was a significant phase in the process by which English society became urbanised and one in which 'England's urban world was becoming notably multi-centred rather than focused upon a single city' [266 p. 10].

It would, however, be a display of perverse anti-metropolitan prejudice to understate the economic, social, political and cultural pre-eminence in England of London throughout the entire early modern period. London's growth in size was rapid in an international as well as in a national context. Fuelled by migration (London's birth rate always lagged behind its death rate even in the wealthier parishes) the capital expanded to 200,000 by 1600, 400,000 by 1650 and 575,000 by 1700. The great fire of 1666 was a prelude to the rebuilding of the City, while the population of London spilled outside the City boundaries both to the east and west. By 1650 only Paris among west European cities was as big as London; during the next century London left even Paris behind. The impact on the English economy of London's growth continued throughout the early modern period [*Doc. 35*]. The capital's demands for food and raw materials influenced many agricultural regions of the country and were a crucial factor in the commercialisation and specialisation of English agriculture in the early modern period [271].

London's impact on English society was no less important. The rapid population growth of the capital and the influx of poor migrants brought difficult social problems for the City authorities, but, despite contemporary fears of dire consequences [*Doc. 34*], there were few major outbreaks of disorders in early modern London. There is a need to be careful not to exaggerate London's stability as some historians have done [273; 276]. London had serious social problems. But these never got seriously out of hand, largely because of the effective measures to defuse social tensions taken by a united metropolitan elite, especially in the later sixteenth and early seventeenth centuries [258]. As a result, London was able to develop as the country's major cultural centre. In the later sixteenth and early seventeenth centuries its shops, entertainment facilities (like Paris Gardens in Southwark), schools (like Westminster and St Paul's) and the Inns of Court, attracted members of the landed elite to stay in the capital during the winter months, the first signs of a London 'season' [270]. The metropolis, in short, came to be an important focus of fashion in a range of fields from clothes to ideas, and therefore a means by which they could be diffused throughout the whole country. The period after the mid-seventeenth century saw a significant acceleration of the process with the rapid growth in London of coffee houses (by the reign of Queen Anne it has been estimated that there were 12,000), taverns and political clubs, which acted as forums for the discussion and dissemination of ideas by word of mouth and also in print.

There was a boom in the publication of newspapers and magazines from the late seventeenth century onwards and these were passed from hand to hand in the coffee houses and clubs of London. The capital's role as a centre of national culture must be put alongside its function as 'an engine of economic growth' and its better-known importance as the fulcrum of the legal and political world of early modern England.

It was not until the middle of the seventeenth century that the development of provincial towns came to rival London's pre-eminence. It is significant that historians are deeply divided on the functions and fortunes of provincial towns in the century or so before that date (contrast the views in 2 and 265). Although there is a growing agreement that there was an urban crisis in the middle of the sixteenth century (for many reasons including the fact that much industry moved out of towns into the countryside), that consensus collapses on the questions of the severity and duration of the urban crisis. One of the central issues currently dividing urban historians is whether or not the recovery of provincial towns began in the late sixteenth and early seventeenth centuries. The varying approaches to that problem reflect the diverse evidence that some towns were prospering and others were not during that period, but they ought not to obscure the generally sluggish trend in provincial urban developments before the mid-seventeenth century.

It is not until after 1650 that the evidence becomes clearer and less ambiguous, so that one can write with more confidence about a new phase of urban growth, which has encouraged Peter Borsay to characterise the later seventeenth and early eighteenth centuries as a period which saw 'the English urban renaissance' [260]. In particular, three types of provincial towns underwent a period of rapid growth and development. The first of these were 'county' towns which developed as 'little Londons', as social and political centres of fairly wide regions, and which were usually the places where county assizes and quarter sessions were held, like Durham, York, Lincoln, Stamford, Norwich, King's Lynn, Bury St Edmunds in eastern England, Chester, Preston, Shrewsbury in the west and Maidstone and Salisbury in the south. The second are spa towns like Bath, Tunbridge Wells, Harrogate, and Hampstead and Islington in London, which expanded along with the fashion for taking their waters. Thirdly, the period saw the expansion of towns which developed special economic functions as industrial and dockyard towns and ports. The main manufacturing towns were those pro-ducing staple products, like the textile towns, Manchester, Leeds and Norwich [*Doc. 30*], metal-manufacturing towns, Sheffield and Birmingham, and hosiery towns, Derby, Leicester and Nottingham [*Doc. 29*]. The principal expanding ports were in the west (Liverpool, Whitehaven and Bristol) and north east (Newcastle, Sunderland and Hull), although the dockyard towns (Chatham, Portsmouth and Plymouth) provided some urban growth points in the south.

That the century after 1650 is such an important one in the process of urban development in England is partly explained by contemporary economic trends. The prosperity which characterises the English overseas trade 'revolution' and the diversification of English manufacturing in the century after 1650 began to shift the economic centre of the country gradually away from the south and south east to the Midlands, north and north west. This is reflected in the broad pattern of provincial urban expansion outlined above. Equally important in bringing this about was the increase in agricultural production in England in the later seventeenth and early eighteenth centuries, which released a greater percentage of the population from the business of producing food. This is reflected in the continuing pattern of migration into towns throughout the period, despite the slight fall in the national population in the late seventeenth century. During the seventeenth century the population of England rose by 23 per cent, while the urban population increased by 100 per cent. Urban expansion, too, is a reflection of the rising real incomes of many people that have been analysed earlier. As the economy thrived, so groups of people emerged who had rising cultural and social aspirations, which points to a final, allied, feature of urban growth in the later seventeenth and early eighteenth centuries.

The growth of provincial towns after 1650 was not merely a quantitative, but was also a qualitative one: the development of an urban culture and consciousness [260]. This is reflected in the spate of improvements both in public amenities in many towns in this period – street-widening and cleaning, sewerage and water supply schemes, for example – and in public buildings, like hospitals, town halls and churches. A further manifestation of this emerging distinctive 'urban culture' and of the burgeoning national prosperity that underpinned it is the development of organised leisure facilities in towns. J. H. Plumb has argued that there took place in the later seventeenth and early eighteenth centuries what he calls 'the commercialization of leisure' [286]. Many leisure activities that had hitherto been available only to the very rich were now opened up to a wider audience. The growth of a relatively cheap, popular press, publishing devices like the production of serialised 'part' books, and circulating and subscription libraries brought the printed word to more people than ever before. Provincial theatres and the building of assembly rooms reflected the wider audience in towns for things like musical concerts and art exhibitions. Sports, too, like horse-racing, cricket and prizefighting, underwent a similar process of popularisation and commercialisation. It is important not to exaggerate the size of the audience that was catered for. It was restricted to the upper and middling social groups in early modern society. Yet these innovations mark a crucial step towards a situation in which popular tastes (rather than the patronage of a small elite) influenced the development of the arts and related leisure and cultural activities.

A 'CONSUMER SOCIETY'?

In the late seventeenth century some contemporaries began to comment on the fact that goods normally restricted to the upper landed classes were being bought, worn and eaten by a much wider range of people. For many, this was something to be condemned as a sign of growing indulgence in luxurious and wasteful expenditure [*Doc. 36*]. Others, however, began to be persuaded that it might not necessarily be an unwelcome development on the grounds that home demand was capable of fuelling economic change and expansion [*Doc. 37*]. This theme – that rising domestic demand for manufactured goods, luxuries, services and entertainment was an important contributor to economic growth – has much to recommend it. In the early modern period there emerged a society in England that was wealthy enough to provide the demand necessary to encourage the rapid growth of the English manufacturing economy before – indeed as an essential precondition of – the later industrialisation associated with the Industrial Revolution [39; 28; 284].

Some of the evidence for the emergence of 'a consumer society' has already been seen in the changes in material conditions of individual social groups in the early modern period: the growth in numbers and wealth of landed gentlemen, larger farmers, merchants, manufacturers and professional groups, together with the possibility that not all small farmers and landless labourers suffered the sharp deterioration in economic fortunes that some have described. Even before 1650 English agriculture had begun to meet the challenge of rising demand for food from an expanding population with a fair amount of success and there was sufficient demand for non-food items to support a vast array of consumer industries. These 'projects' were partly made possible by the 'development (from the sixteenth century onwards) of a consumer society that embraced not only the nobility and gentry and substantial yeomen, but included humble peasants, labourers, servants, as well' [288 *p. 179*]. Many of the new consumer industries originated in schemes promoted by the Crown and by those close to it in the sixteenth and early seventeenth centuries. (Not all the projects approved by the Crown were as bogus or as ill-conceived commercially as the Cockayne Project of 1614.) Yet they could not have been successful without a substantial consumer demand for their products.

That demand for manufactured products and services rose before the middle of the seventeenth century is only a probability given the present state of knowledge; for the century after 1650, however, it is a certainty. In the later seventeenth and early eighteenth centuries there was 'a more substantial and more widely distributed reserve of disposable income [in England] than anywhere else in Europe' [33 *p. 197*]. Consequently, ordinary English men and women began to eat and wear a wider range of commodities than ever before. The development of cattle-rearing on a large scale in specialised regions like the Surrey and Kent Wealds and the heavy clay soils of the Midlands (especially Leicestershire) suggests that there was an increase in meat consumption. Moreover, more people began to eat wheat rather than other grains that were felt to be poorer, such as barley and rye. It is also clear that from the mid-seventeenth century overseas trade began to supply new types of goods for people to eat and to wear. Many of the products of the new American, Caribbean and Far Eastern trades were initially re-exported in large quantities to Europe. But increasingly many of these commodities, like sugar and tobacco, were retained, sold and consumed in England, while at the same time their prices fell. By 1750 nearly one million hundred-weights of sugar (nearly 90 per cent of the total amount imported) were retained for the domestic market. Similarly, by 1750 about three million pounds in weight of tea (again about 90 per cent of the total imported) were bought and drunk in England. At the same time new textile goods from the East – mostly cheap calicoes, muslins and silks from India – began to flood into England.

Much is known about the value of these products from overseas because they are recorded in customs accounts (from 1696 the medieval series of accounts, which was interrupted in 1601, was resumed). One can be less certain about the quantities of untaxed and therefore unrecorded native products – pottery, glassware, metal goods, for example – that were bought in this period. But the proliferation of consumer industries at this time suggests a rapidly expanding domestic market. There was, for example, a dramatic increase in the output and consumption of spirits, beer and porter in the early eighteenth century. For national statistics of the extent of the home market one has again to rely on King's figures. In 1688 he reckoned that the value of all goods produced in England was £48 million, of which £44.6 million (93 per cent in value) was sold on the home market [342].

As a wider range of goods became available in early modern England, so better methods of distributing them were developed [30; 45]. The period before 1650 was not devoid of improvements. That there were over 272 services per week by road carriers from London to most counties of England and Wales in 1637 suggests that the 'binding mud' interpretation of pre-industrial road transport needs abandoning. Goods were carried by wagons, packhorses and on the hoof along roads and drovers' routes that seemed primitive and impassable to urban dwellers like Celia Fiennes and Daniel Defoe (as well as to some modern historians). But it was the late seventeenth and early eighteenth centuries which saw the biggest improvement in internal transport and communications before the heyday of canals and turnpike trusts in the late eighteenth century. There was an aggregate increase in road services out of London of 36.5 per cent in the period 1637–81 and an increase of 64.3 per cent between 1681 and 1715 [44]. Yet it was water transport that was more important, especially in the carriage of bulky goods; like the coastal trade in coal from the north east or the busy trade in west Midlands metalwares down the river Severn. The growing demand for goods of all kinds produced a rash of river improvements and early canal schemes in the later seventeenth and early eighteenth centuries.

Symptomatic of the growth of a consumer society was the development of retail shops, not only in London but in many provincial towns and villages [279; 285]. Petty chapmen continued to play a crucial role in the distributive trades. Indeed Margaret Spufford goes so far as to claim that the range of drapery and haberdashery they carried in the later seventeenth century 'brought about a minor revolution in domestic comfort amongst the poorest in society for whom inventories were made' [287 *p. 146*]. But the history of shopping begins in the sixteenth century and gradually the great medieval fairs, like that held annually at Stourbridge in

Worcestershire, were transformed into agricultural and wholesale markets, and metropolitan and provincial shops began to appear to compete with pedlars and itinerant tradesmen for the retail trade. The early years of shops are, not surprisingly, difficult to chart because few shopkeepers left records. But, fortunately, some did. James Backhouse of Kirkby Lonsdale in Westmorland was one. He died in 1578 leaving stock which included Spanish silks, French garters, Norwich lace, Oxford gloves and Turkey purses [45]. The two best-known shopkeepers of the late seventeenth century (well known because they wrote autobiographies) are the Lancastrians Roger Lowe of Leigh and William Stout of Lancaster [*Doc. 38*], both of whom stocked a wide range of goods of English, colonial and foreign origins [344; 349]. It is not until the early eighteenth century that evidence accumulates indicating the rapid spread of provincial shops, some advertising their wares in local newspapers. But it is likely that this was pre-dated by a growth of real wealth, changing consumption patterns and the existence of shops during the previous century.

The diffusion of wealth in early modern England is reflected best of all in probate inventories (the lists of goods left in their houses by people who had just died) and in buildings. The best statistical study of inventories is by J. Marshall, who looked at 1,550 Cumbrian inventories, half dating from 1661 to 1690 and half from 1721 to 1750 and discovered that the mean value of inventories rose from £71.23 in the first period to £124.72 in the second, a rise of about 75 per cent [62]. Other less statistically based studies (for example, of the Vale of Berkeley [55], the east Midlands and Norfolk [37]) support this conclusion by pointing to the growing quantities of linen, plate, furnishings and luxury imports recorded in households during this period and especially from the middle of the seventeenth century. Perhaps even more conclusive is the work of R. Machin on housebuilding [283], which substantially modifies W. G. Hoskins's long-established thesis that the period between 1575 and 1625 was an exceptionally active one in the history of English domestic architecture. So many new farmhouses were built and existing ones extended and improved in that period that Hoskins described it as an era of 'Great Rebuilding', after which housebuilding slumped [282]. Machin's investigations challenge Hoskins's chronology and open up the possibility that the later sixteenth and early seventeenth centuries were not a peak period in the history of domestic building but were part of a longer period of growth which extended from the mid-sixteenth century: 'Quantitatively the period from 1660 to 1739 was far more important, with every decade producing more dated houses than even the peak period of the pre-Civil War period.' In fact 'the outstanding decade for dated houses was the 1690s' [283 p. 37]. In north Warwickshire from the mid-seventeenth century 'special function' rooms, parlours, living rooms and bedrooms, began to be built as houses got bigger and more comfortable to live in. People there also spent an increasing portion of their wealth on items of personal consumption and use than on items for production, like farm implements. Whereas in 1600–19 the percentages spent on consumption goods and goods for production purposes had been 27 and 73 per cent respectively, by 1680–91 the comparable figures are 48 and 52 per cent [85].

Already before the end of the seventeenth century there can be seen the outlines of a consumer society that was even more obvious after 1700. 'There was a consumer revolution in the eighteenth century. More and more men and women than ever before in human history enjoyed the experience of acquiring material possessions – objects which had been the privileged possession of the rich came to be within the reach of a larger part of society than ever before, and, for the first time, to be within the legitimate aspirations of almost all of it' [283 p. 1].

PART THREE: CHANGING IDEAS

As well as major changes in material conditions and related alterations in the framework of English society, the early modern period also saw important developments in people's ideas, attitudes and beliefs. Three of these changes stand out: an expansion in educational opportunities and growth of literacy; the triumph of Protestantism as the official ideology of the English Church and people; and the spread of modern scientific principles and rational, empirical methodology. As will be seen, some of these intellectual developments do not mark as 'revolutionary' a break with the past as may at first sight appear; nor did they affect the attitudes, beliefs and modes of thought of everyone with equal force. As might be expected, there was a significant difference between the impact these developments had on the intelligentsia and on the mass of people. This difference underlines the gulf that *already* existed between learned and popular cultures.

One of the most controversial problems about the impact of ideas on society in the early modern period, however, is whether they widened that gulf. It has been argued that there was a 'growing cultural differentiation within English society which was one of the most significant developments of the age' [67 *p. 184*]. The influence of new ideas was confined to the wealthy and prosperous, who consequently became increasingly distinct in their attitudes and modes of thought from the mass of the population. In this view the most significant general trend in the history of ideas in the early modern period was the development of a gulf between 'patrician' or 'elite' on the one hand and 'plebeian' cultures on the other [290; 307].

There is no doubt that many of the ideas that gained currency in this period were absorbed and discussed in learned and non-learned ways. What is less certain is whether these differences coincided with social divisions and whether they were as marked as it has been claimed they were. As will be seen, a considerable minority of ordinary people in early modern England could read, if not write, and were not culturally isolated. Moreover, despite the different ways in which new ideas were treated, inherent in them were general concepts which were shared by proponents of both the learned and the popular cultures. Many of these concepts are those that typified the intellectual climate of modern Britain in the nineteenth and twentieth centuries, which provides a justification for seeing the early modern period (and especially the period after 1650) as of equal significance in the forging of modern ideas and attitudes as it is in the emergence of a more recognisably modern framework of society. Yet it must be emphasised that in the early modern period these concepts had not yet triumphed over traditional ideas. In the mental worlds of such diverse early modern individuals as Newton [176] and Defoe [174] 'modern' and 'traditional' concepts were inseparable. The intellectual climate of the country between the mid-sixteenth and mid-eighteenth centuries, like its social structure, was neither 'medieval' nor 'modern'; it was distinctively 'early modern'.

10 EDUCATION AND LITERACY

There is no doubt that a considerable expansion in educational opportunities occurred in late sixteenth- and early seventeenth-century England [294; 299]. Judging by the evidence of licences to teach issued by bishops, 'petty' schools, which were local schools teaching the basic 'three Rs', existed in many parishes by the end of the sixteenth century, and, in addition, many grammar schools were founded to teach a classically-based curriculum. It has been estimated that between 1560 and 1640 over £293,000 was given by individuals to establish grammar schools and that 142 new ones were established between 1603 and 1649. The impression of educational expansion in Elizabethan and early Stuart England is confirmed by a parallel growth in higher education, as new colleges were founded at Oxford and Cambridge and a university education, together with a period of legal study at one of the Inns of Court in London – 'the third university' – became a normal part of the career of young gentlemen [229]. Such developments, moreover, are probably only part of a more broadly based educational expansion, since it is likely that many schools and teachers existed that were unlicensed and therefore unrecorded.

However, there are many reasons to doubt whether these developments are part of an 'educational revolution' that allegedly took place between 1560 and 1640 [305]. For one thing, the explosion of source material from about the mid-sixteenth century reflects only a new concern with record-keeping and educational standardisation and therefore it ought not to obscure the growing provision of schools and university colleges that took place in the fifteenth and early sixteenth centuries [300]. The Reformation dislocated this process slightly as some chantry schools were closed as part of the Dissolution, but these closures were everywhere balanced by the foundation or re-foundation of many schools, often called 'King Edward VI' schools. Moreover, not only did the

Elizabethan and early Stuart period witness the continuation of a longer process of educational expansion; it is also likely that this continued in the century after 1660. It is true that influential contemporary opinion at the Restoration blamed the radicalism and regicide of the mid-seventeenth century on increasing educational opportunities and advocated educational cuts as a recipe for social order [*Doc. 39*]. Many since then have argued that the Restoration did mark the beginning of a long period of educational regression and decay [306]. Yet these contemporary and later views distort what actually happened. In many parts of the country new schools continued to be founded in the later seventeenth century [225]. In Charles II's reign eighty new grammar schools were founded. Moreover, both Anglican and Dissenter interests began to found schools as part of a long denominational struggle for the control of education which continued in the nineteenth century and beyond. From the 1690s charity schools began to be established by Anglicans, supported by the Church of England's Society for the Propagation of Christian Knowledge, while Dissenting Academies were established by those Protestants excluded from attending the universities after the Restoration [296]. Alongside these, private schools of many types were set up in the later seventeenth century, many of which, like the Dissenting Academies, taught a wide range of subjects, not only classical studies but mathematics, science and foreign languages [295; 298].

Recent work on literacy levels suggests that the impact on English society of this long period of educational expansion ought not to be exaggerated [293]. This work is based largely on signatures. Although the ability to sign one's name is obviously not a foolproof indication of the ability to read, in a period (unlike our own) when it was common for children to be taught to read before they learned to write, signatures probably are as good a guide to literacy as anything else (indeed, given the pattern of teaching reading and writing, statistics based on signatures may understate levels of literacy). Work on a large sample of signatures from different parts of England has led to the conclusion that overall literacy rates rose in early modern England (and especially in the later sixteenth century). But this conclusion has to be qualified by the fact that literacy levels throughout the period were higher in towns and among men, wealthy landowners, merchants and shopkeepers than they were in the countryside and among women, farmers, craftsmen and the labouring classes.

Yet there are grounds for believing that early modern England was not split into two nations, the literate wealthy and 'middling sort' and the illiterate poor. Reading did become part of the popular culture of early modern England [297]. This was a period when there were many incentives for ordinary people to want to learn to read, including the need to read documents (like apprenticeship indentures or manorial court rolls) that affected their economic lives. Religion too was a prime motive for people to become literate [*Doc. 41*]. The emphasis of Protestantism on Bible-reading accounts for the evidence of the ownership of the Bible (and therefore probably the ability to read it) among a wide spectrum of English society. Religious literature of other sorts, like catechisms and religious ballads, also formed the staple of the popular literature of early modern England. Of Samuel Pepys's extensive collection of 'chapbooks' designed for a popular audience, 24 per cent are 'small godly books' with titles like *The Doors of Salvation Opened*, as well as abridged versions of Bunyan's *The Pilgrim's Progress*. These kinds of works were part of a wider popular literature published in many forms: pamphlets, small books, ballads and almanacs, embracing many 'merry' themes, including courtship, sex, chivalry, as well as more serious themes of history and religion [291; 302–4]. After the lapse of the Licensing Act in 1695 the production of newspapers and other types of political journalism also expanded, so that 'by 1700 reading of newspapers had become a settled habit in England and . . . the habit was not confined to a ruling minority'. What is more, ordinary people, like Thomas Tryon, a tiler's son, often learned to read at home or at their place of work rather than at school [*Doc. 40*]. Their existence must qualify the view that society in the early modern period was divided into a literate elite and an illiterate poor who were barred from sharing in the culture of their 'betters'.

11 THE IMPACT OF PROTESTANTISM

1550–1625

The emphasis on literacy to enable everyone to read the Bible was one of many characteristics which gradually became a more important part of English cultural life after the Reformation, when Protestantism became the official religion of the English state to which everyone was compelled to conform. The task of bringing about a Protestant reformation in the minds and lives of people was, however, much slower than the passage through parliament of Acts of Uniformity and Supremacy.

One obstacle was the strength of popular attachment to Catholicism which for much of the sixteenth century was far greater than many have thought [316–17; 320–1; 325]. The Reformation began as an Act of State by Henry VIII and his advisers and the close relationship between Catholicism and the routine of English parochial life could not be extinguished overnight. In general, Protestant evangelists had most success in the first years after the Reformation in the southern and eastern counties of England and they bemoaned the fact that the north and west were 'the dark corners of the land'. Yet even in many areas of the south and east, Catholicism survived into the late sixteenth century, especially in areas where it received the protection of powerful landed gentlemen. Catholicism survived in early modern England as 'a seigneurial religion', especially from the late 1570s when English missionary priests trained in continental seminaries began to arrive in secret in England, often to be employed as officials in the houses of landed gentlemen [309–10; 323]. They brought with them the literature and ideas of the Catholic Church of the Counter-Reformation, the post-Tridentine Catholicism that elsewhere in Europe was proving to be very successful in combating the Protestant Reformation. In England, however, their success was slight. Popular Catholicism, the roots of which lay in the pre-Reformation period, slowly declined.

This was not inevitable given early sixteenth-century evidence of the central place of the Catholic Church in popular culture, but popular Catholicism after the Reformation was given little support by wealthy Catholic landowners and missionary priests. Therefore, by the early seventeenth century, whereas post-Tridentine Catholicism survived among a handful of wealthy Catholics in England who maintained an introverted, 'quasi-monastic', politically quiescent life-style, support for popular Catholicism dwindled until the total number of English Catholics was tiny. In 1604 Catholics made up 1.5 per cent of the population of Yorkshire and this probably represents the overall percentage of Catholics in England by this stage.

A more persistent obstacle than Catholicism to the task of Protestant Reformation was a traditional pattern of magical beliefs that provided alternative explanations to those offered by the Church for events – sudden deaths and other tragedies, for example – that it was difficult to account for rationally. Belief in magic was prevalent in England in the later sixteenth and early seventeenth centuries and formed part of popular culture, distinct from the mystical beliefs which it will be seen were current in intellectual circles at this time (see Chapter 12) [326]. The evidence of a growing number of witchcraft cases before the courts in this period, and especially in the 1580s and 1590s, reveals that belief in maleficent magic was widespread, as was belief in 'white', beneficial magic [322]. In many English villages people, variously described as 'cunning', 'wise men' and 'wizards', existed who, it was believed, had the power to heal, recover stolen property and perform other good works. It is possible that belief in magic had always existed in England, but the Reformation, by abolishing such things as the confessional role of priests and the healing capacity of saints, holy water and relics, undoubtedly encouraged it. The Reformation 'denied the value of the Church's rituals and referred the believer back to the unpredictable mercies of God. If religion continued to be regarded by its adherents as a source of power, then it was a power that was patently much diminished' [326 *p. 77*].

Indifference to religion, too, was another common complaint of Protestant evangelists that was perhaps not new. They complained constantly of the 'ungodly' behaviour of those who attended church and those that did not, signalling out specifically for condemnation the inhabitants of the 'forest-pasture' communities [*Doc. 6*]. Given all this, it is not surprising that the progress of the Protestant Reformation at the grass roots level was slow and uneven.

Yet by the reign of James I great steps forward had been made and the Protestant Church had usurped Catholicism's central position in the lives of most English men and women. Traditionally, Puritans have been taken to be the most significant example of the new Protestant culture that became slowly dominant in Elizabethan and early Stuart England. Yet this is misleading, since it exaggerates both the separateness of Puritans from other Protestants and their overall importance and typicality in this period. Many of the characteristics often described as 'Puritan' were shared by many English Protestants and became typical of the new common Protestant culture that was established in England by the early seventeenth century [311–14]. Some of these have already been seen, like attitudes to the family, literacy and Bible-reading. These were part of a wide Protestant consensus on the importance of the direct relationship between individuals and God rather than through the intermediary of a priest. Therefore the prime duty of church ministers came to be expounding the Bible in sermons rather than carrying out ceremonial and sacramental functions. The Gospel should be spread by preaching and it was important, therefore, that the clergy should be educated enough to preach sermons that would be effective in propagating the Gospel to the 'dark corners of the land'. Preaching, an educated clergy, literate congregations and sermonoriented church services came to be the essence of English Protestantism, along with a predestinarian theology which stressed that an individual's fate after death is preordained, since the Elect are already chosen; a belief that the Sabbath was a special day to be set apart specifically for worship and religious education; and an intense anti-Catholicism.

Of all these common characteristics of Protestantism by the early seventeenth century, the last is the most important in binding English Protestants together. It is also the most difficult aspect of early modern Protestantism to understand, given the fact that Catholicism was losing its hold on English people. Yet the belief that popery was a potent force of evil was so strong largely because it was based on a powerful worldview, popularised in one of the most influential books written in this period, John Foxe's *Acts and Monuments (The Book of Martyrs)*. Foxe's book started from the notion that the world was involved in a continuing struggle between the forces of Christ and of Antichrist and that, since the Reformation, Antichrist was Rome and the battle against it was led by the Protestant nations of Europe. Some English Protestants – though by no means all – even argued that England was the Elect

Nation chosen by God for this task, that would eventually climax in the defeat of Antichrist and the establishment of the Millennium, prophesied in the Books of the Old Testament, when King Jesus would return to earth to rule. Such a view gained cogency in the early seventeenth century through events in Europe, as European Protestantism seemed threatened by the rising tide of Counter-Reformation Catholicism in the Thirty Years' War.

These were all aspects of a Protestant ideology that were not peculiar to Puritans. Puritans, however, did exist in the late sixteenth and early seventeenth centuries as a group of people who felt themselves to be different from other Protestants and who did have a distinctive life-style that is reflected in the diary of Lady Margaret Hoby or the autobiography of Richard Baxter [334; 340] [*Doc. 42*]. They often called themselves, not Puritans (which is what their enemies called them) but 'the godly'. They were people whose attitudes to life and death were influenced more strongly than others by Protestant principles. They lived their daily lives at a high level of spiritual intensity, spent long periods in introspection and self-examination in order to confirm that they were chosen to be of the Elect, and were more militant than most in wanting to rid the Church of remnants of popery, to spread the Gospel and to bring about a 'reformation of manners' by attacking drunkenness, swearing, sexual misdemeanours, alehouse disorders and profanation of the Sabbath. These 'godly' Puritans, however, were only a minority in England in the early seventeenth century, and a minority that was not confined to any one social group (despite what is often assumed). Puritans in Elizabethan and early Stuart England came from all social groups and not just from 'the middling sort'. They ranged from peers like the third earl of Huntingdon, 'the Puritan earl' [173], to the humble villagers of Warbleton in Sussex and Cranbrook in Kent who gave their children names of 'godly signification' like Sure-trust and Sin-deny [328]. Nor were all 'ungodly' Protestants poor people. 'Is there any reason to suppose that the young people of Elizabethan Kent who gadded to dances were denizens of some natural "Third World" and subject to greater deprivation than their neighbours who gadded to sermons?' [312 *p. 220*].

Above all, 'godly' Protestants were fewer in number than those Protestants who, by the early seventeenth century, did not study the tenets of Protestantism with the fervour of the 'godly' and who were less sure of the finer points of theology. Most Protestants were by this time, however, very attached to the outward practices of the post-Reformation episcopal English Church to which everyone was obliged to belong – a Church that conducted its services according to the Book of Common Prayer promulgated in 1559 and that celebrated the traditional festivals of Easter, Whitsuntide and Christmas. The Rogation week perambulations of parishes prescribed in the 1562 Book of Homilies encapsulated the way in which the Church came to be 'locked into the country calendar' [121 *p. 80*]. Attempts to alter that Church in a Puritan direction in the 1640s produced the outcry seen in petitions to parliament in 1641–2 and in the Clubman movement of 1645 [*Doc. 43*]. The point is underlined by the failure of many parishes to adopt the Puritan reforms of the 1640s abolishing among other things the Book of Common Prayer and Christmas. By this stage the English post-Reformation Church (though in the eyes of the 'godly' only half-reformed) represented a 'rhythm of worship, piety, practice, that had established itself into the Englishman's consciousness and had sunk deep roots in popular culture' [324 *p. 113*].

1625–1750

Before 1625 the evolution of a shared English Protestant culture was more important than differences among Protestants. Slowly after 1625, however, divisions between Protestants widened and eventually came to have a major impact on English society. This process began largely because Charles I adopted a novel form of theology and liturgy – known as Arminianism after one of its principal exponents, a Leyden theologian, Jacobus Arminius – which, after becoming king in 1625, he attempted, with the support of William Laud (Bishop of London and later Archbishop of Canterbury), to impose on the English Church. In so doing, Charles and Laud shattered the delicate unity of English Protestantism between the 'godly' and others that had been maintained in the Elizabethan–Jacobean Church. This came about because some Protestants – especially the 'godly' – found it difficult to accept the Church under Laud and so began to separate from it.

What was there about Arminianism that caused some Protestants to take such a drastic step? Arminianism came to be seen as a direct challenge to the type of English Church that had become widely accepted by the early seventeenth century [327]. Whether doctrinally this is so is a matter for debate, but certainly for some English Protestants the Arminian doctrine of free will seemed to be a fundamental attack on the doctrine of predestinarianism. More importantly, the Arminians' belief in the indiscriminate granting of

God's grace led them to emphasise the importance of sacramental and ceremonial aspects of the church service and to downgrade Bible-reading, preaching and sermons. What is more, Arminians saw no reason to set aside the Sabbath for religious worship and meditation and they actively encouraged Sunday sports and festivities, as did the Declaration of Sports issued by Charles I in 1633. Consequently, although Laud was not a Catholic, to many his views seemed to be as near to Catholicism as made no difference. This was bad enough, given the strength of contemporary anti-Catholicism. But what is more, Laud attempted to increase the power of bishops: he encouraged ecclesiastical courts to prosecute those who committed 'whoredom, incest, drunkenness, swearing, ribaldry and usury' regardless of their social origins, and he began a campaign against the lay control of tithes. Arminianism came to be seen to represent a growing tide of popery and an increasing interference by clerics in secular affairs. Charles and Laud had turned the English Church away from the mainstream position it had occupied in post-Reformation England, and in so doing they effectively created English Protestant Dissent.

During the 1630s it is not known how many people withdrew from the Church. Most who did so probably emigrated to the newly established colonies in New England. After 1640, however, whole congregations separated from the Church. The first one recorded is the Broadmead congregation in Bristol, which in 1640 decided to 'come forth of the world and worship the Lord more purely' [329 *p. 71*] by establishing their own gathered church separate from the parish church. During the next two decades, following the collapse of the ecclesiastical hierarchy and its control, religious sects proliferated with a bewildering range of doctrinal beliefs and practices – adult and infant baptism, free will, predestinarianism – and with an equally bewildering range of names, from the Particular and General Baptists, Presbyterians, Independents and Quakers, to the Grindletonians, Muggletonians and Ranters. As yet, though, the divisions between these groups were not rigid. With the collapse of censorship in the revolutionary decades it was possible for individuals to experiment with different beliefs, to become (as they said) 'seekers'. This fluidity, as well as the intellectual and spiritual excitement of the period, is conveyed in Lawrence Clarkson's autobiography [*Doc. 44*]. Gradually, however, denominational boundaries began to harden. In 1656 an Assembly of General Baptists took place in London and five Associations of Particular Baptists existed in England in the 1650s [329].

When Oliver Cromwell became Protector in 1653 one of his aims was to bring together most of these groups under the umbrella of the state Church. The apparatus of state control in the Cromwellian Church was less awesome than that which had existed before 1640 – the Act of Uniformity was abolished in the 1650s. But in other respects Cromwell aimed to establish a Church, like the Elizabethan–Jacobean Church, that was broad and tolerant enough to encompass a wide variety of Protestant groups. Nor did the attempt end with Cromwell's death in 1658. In the eighteen months after the Restoration in 1660 Charles II attempted (at the Worcester and Savoy House conferences) to restore a comprehensive Church of the type that had existed before 1625 [319].

But by 1660 this was impossible. In only some respects was the Church that was restored in 1660 like the old Church. Bishops returned, as did the Book of Common Prayer and the traditional Christian festivals. However, one change that the events of the 1640s and 1650s brought about was to identify Dissenters with radicalism and regicide, and 'Dissent is Sedition' became a powerful political slogan at the Restoration. Even before the Cavalier Parliament met, the Anglican Church was restored at the grass roots. When the Cavalier Parliament did meet in 1661 it began to enact a series of laws – 'the Clarendon Code' – which imposed severe penalties on non-Anglicans, confirming that the restored Church was much narrower and less tolerant than that which had developed under Elizabeth I and James I [*Doc. 45*]. The 1660s and 1670s witnessed the greatest period of religious persecution in English history. Nor was that the end of Anglican opposition to Dissenters, which flared up again in the 1690s and early 1700s, as has been seen earlier.

Yet Protestant Dissent survived 'the period of great persecution'. Paradoxically, some Dissenting sects thrived rather than dwindled in conditions of persecution, largely because persecution encouraged spiritual enrichment. It is no coincidence that this period produced great classics of Dissenting literature like William Penn's *No Cross, No Cross* and John Bunyan's *The Pilgrim's Progress*. On the other hand, it is equally clear that the Clarendon Code was not always put into practice with as much vigour as it might have been. Not all Anglican magistrates were willing to penalise Dissenters who they knew were not the seditious radicals they were often said to be. At times, too, especially during the reign of James II, the dangers of Catholicism forced Protestants to close ranks, as they did in 1688–9. One outcome of these events was the Toleration Act of 1689, which allowed limited freedom of worship to some (if not all) Protestant Dissenters. So Dissent survived and by the early eighteenth century English Protestantism was irrevocably divided between Anglicans and Nonconformists. One consequence was to create a new (and permanent) divide in English society as well: between the Church and the Chapel.

It is ironic that one can now see that in reality the threat posed to the Church by Dissent, which had prevented the establishment of a comprehensive Protestant Church, was not as great as it seemed to be. Dissenters were still only a tiny fraction of the population: about 6 per cent in the second decade of the eighteenth century is the most recent estimate [329]. Moreover, Dissent seems gradually to have lost its spiritual vigour. This coincided with the beginnings of a long association between Dissenters and manufacturing and commercial enterprise exemplified by Quaker families like the Barclays, Lloyds, Whitbreads and Darbys, brought about by their exclusion from politics and polite society. It is no coincidence that groups like the Quakers and Baptists lost much of their early evangelical zeal at exactly this time. Yet Anglicanism was not immune either from a general drift away from 'enthusiasm' in religion in the later seventeenth and early eighteenth centuries. This is most clearly exemplified by the growth of Latitudinarianism in the English Church. Latitudinarian divines, who slowly captured key offices in the Church hierarchy, stressed rational arguments rather than revelation and faith as the basis of their Christian beliefs. They defended religion rationally and coolly. Reasonableness in religion grew, and with it religion lost its central position in some people's lives. 'Religion', said the earl of Chesterfield in the early eighteenth century, 'is by no means a proper subject in a mixed company'. Such a view understates the continuing influence of Protestantism in English life by this stage, but it indicates a falling away from the kind of religious passion that had characterised life in the late sixteenth and early seventeenth centuries. English society by the early eighteenth century had become secularised: a social change that was inextricably bound up with the Scientific Revolution.

12 THE SCIENTIFIC REVOLUTION

The Scientific Revolution of the sixteenth and seventeenth centuries had implications beyond what is now known as 'science' [330–33]. The discoveries of the 'natural philosophers' – the scientists – of the early modern period came about as part of a major transformation in attitudes and modes of thought among people generally in England and throughout Europe. Gradually the passive acceptance of traditional unchallenged truths – an 'attitude of contemplative resignation' which characterised medieval modes of thought [326 p. 643] – was replaced by the belief that man can change his condition and environment for the better. Slowly in the early modern period the Idea of Progress, which was to become common in Britain in the nineteenth and early twentieth centuries, took root.

Though not all medieval scientists neglected observation and experimentation, the main sources of their beliefs were books written centuries before by Greek philosophers whose assumptions were only minimally influenced by what they saw and what they deduced from practical experiments. Both Galen, who lived in Greece in the second century AD and whose treatises were the basis of academic medicine until the seventeenth century, and his contemporary Ptolemy, whose view of a finite, earth-centred universe was similarly deep-rooted in medieval thought, reached their views largely by theoretical reasoning and logical deduction. Both men (in turn) based many of their ideas on the physics and astronomy of another Greek, Aristotle, who lived in the fourth century BC. Since it was believed that these 'ancients' had discovered the 'truth' about the physical nature of man, his environment and the universe, there was no compulsion to make new discoveries, for it was thought that there was little left of fundamental importance to be discovered. The answers to many problems, it was believed, could be found in the writings of traditional authorities: the works of Greek philosophers, and later medieval commentaries on them.

However, in the early sixteenth century a handful of natural philosophers began a series of investigations which challenged the traditional view of man and his environment. Coincidentally in 1543 two men, who had no contact with each other – Copernicus, a Pole, and Vesalius, an Italian – published treatises which are fundamental in the history of the Scientific Revolution. They attacked, respectively, the Ptolemaic geocentric view of the universe and Galen's anatomical ideas. Moreover, of most importance, unlike the 'ancients', both Vesalius and Copernicus based their conclusions on experimentation and observation rather than on what they had read. Vesalius's description of the human anatomy was written after he had dissected human corpses; and Copernicus's theory that the sun, not the earth, was the centre of the universe was founded on detailed astronomical observations. The ways in which later scientists throughout Europe, including England, developed and expanded the ideas of Vesalius and Copernicus and continued to question the principles and methods of medieval science are well known.

The major British contribution to the Scientific Revolution in the later sixteenth and early seventeenth centuries was in the realms of mathematics and medicine, with the work of John Napier on logarithms and William Oughtred on trigonometry and the discovery by William Harvey of the circulation of the blood. Moreover, Sir Francis Bacon's writings in the early seventeenth century, though they did not have a decisive influence in shaping the new rational and empirical approach, certainly typified the spirit of the Scientific Revolution [*Doc. 46*]. The 1640s and 1650s saw an intensification of empirical research in England, as well as the foundation of scientific clubs in Oxford, Cambridge and London, out of which developed the society which in 1662 became the Royal Society [333]. What contributed to this mid-century scientific progress was not any positive links between Puritanism and science but the fact that the 1640s and 1650s were years of great intellectual excitement which were conducive to discussion of new ideas and methodology. The Restoration did not put an end to this. The last forty years of the seventeenth century have been described as 'arguably one of the most fertile periods in the history of English science' [331 *p. 11*]. Since this was a period that saw, among other things, the publication of works by Robert Boyle, Robert Hooke and Isaac Newton, the description is clearly justified.

Did the Scientific Revolution bring about any changes in English society? The answer is not as clear-cut as it might at first sight appear. First, it would be wrong to assume that the evolution of new scientific principles marked the replacement of the magical and 'irrational' by mechanical and 'rational' explanations of observed phenomena. The Scientific Revolution did not bring about a decline in the belief in magic. Scientists sought explanations in mystical tradition and experience as much as in the mechanical world. The Elizabethan John Dee combined work on mathematics with astrology and spiritualism. William Gilbert, who in 1600 published a treatise demonstrating for the first time the magnetism of the earth by careful experiments, believed that what lay behind the earth's magnetism was the fact that 'the whole universe is animated and that all the globe, all the stars, and also the noble earth, have been governed, since their beginning, by their own appointed souls and have motives of self-conservation'. Gilbert, like others, was greatly influenced by a revival of Neoplatonism and Hermeticism and the belief that spiritual forces lay behind natural phenomena. The fact that Newton spent as much time (if not more) in studying alchemy and the occult as he did on 'modern' subjects like mathematics, astronomy and the composition of light, illustrates that there was no clear decisive break between science and magic in this period [176]. Secondly, the new scientific ideas did not sweep all before them. Before the mid-seventeenth century these ideas were confined to a tiny intellectual elite and, even when the new discoveries became more widely known in the later seventeenth and early eighteenth centuries, they were attacked by intellectual and popular opinion. What fuelled the hostility was disappointment at the wide gap between the aspirations and achievement of those working in pure science and the practical application of those principles [*Doc. 47*]. The connections between the Scientific Revolution and technological progress in agriculture and manufacturing, for example, were slight.

Yet these qualifications ought not to obscure the fact that the general principles and methods practised by natural philosophers were absorbed into the intellectual mainstream of England and came to be shared by a growing number of people in the century after 1650. Problems were increasingly approached by first collecting relevant data and then drawing conclusions from what was found rather than by following traditional solutions. On the contrary, it came to be believed that existing solutions ought to be treated with suspicion until they had been tested rationally. Rational, mechanical causes came increasingly to be preferred in the construction of all kinds of explanations. The new attitudes were not only logical and rational; they were also optimistic, since the new approaches to problems were seen as opening up the possibility of infinite progress in all fields.

The impact of this major change in attitudes and modes of thought that came about fairly rapidly in the later seventeenth and early eighteenth centuries can be seen in many spheres of English society. There is space here to point to only three very different examples. The first is the impact on religious thought. Not only the growth of Latitudinarianism, but also the emergence of deists and other 'freethinkers' was the product of the new rationalistic intellectual climate. Some writers were not always as careful as John Locke in allowing a place for revelation in Christian belief while putting forward reason as its prime source. Others like John Toland in *Christianity not Mysterious* argued that everything in Christianity that could not be explained rationally should be jettisoned. Rational arguments, too, tended towards religious toleration as well as religious indifference. Since, as has been noted above, some Dissenters (like modern dissidents in authoritarian countries) strengthened their attachment to their beliefs in times of persecution, some people began to argue that penal laws did not work and therefore on rational grounds they ought to be abandoned. The second area in which new ideas had a clear impact is in methods of government. A growing number of 'political arithmeticians' including William Petty, John Graunt and Gregory King – whom we would now call statisticians – emerged in the later seventeenth century with the belief that the first and basic step towards solving problems facing governments was the collection of statistics. Once this had been done, they believed, rational solutions could be devised. Much the same was true of the impact of rational thought on attitudes to disease and insanity. Optimism replaced fatalism and some people therefore came to feel that disease could be combated [7; 91].

Attitudes do not, of course, change overnight. In the course of reconstructing the mental world of Daniel Defoe [1660–1731] Peter Earle comments that 'man in the world of Defoe was in a rather confused state. On the one hand stood worldly rational man, the student of natural law, the survivor at all costs who must succeed here and now on earth. But man, too, was the pilgrim seeking salvation, subject to divine providence and bombarded in his dreams and even more on the highway by the apparitions of good and bad spirits' [174 *pp. 43–4*]. But in the period covered by Defoe's life there developed a discernible secularisation of thought and an optimistic faith in the power of man to change society and conditions of life for the better.

PART FOUR: ASSESSMENT

It is not difficult to find aspects of English society in 1750 that had not changed substantially since 1550. It was still an agrarian society in which most people lived and worked on the land. The rhythm of daily life was still influenced greatly by the success or failure of the harvest, and poverty remained a major problem. Wealth was unequally distributed during this whole period and, despite the shock waves during the English Revolution, the power of the Crown, Church and aristocracy remained dominant. 'Revisionist tracts' are not necessary to prove that point [11]. Patriarchalism and deference retained their hold on social relationships in the community; nor were there major changes in the structure of the family or in relationships between members of the family. Moreover, many of the economic developments of early modern England took place within, and did not break the mould of, the traditional framework of the domestic economy.

Yet to isolate these and other elements of continuity would be to miss the fact that during the early modern period major changes did take place in English society, transforming it into one that was not only more recognisably modern than it had been in 1550 but also, of more importance, different in certain key respects from contemporary societies in Scotland, Ireland and parts of continental Europe. Unlike many other countries English society came to be characterised by a three-decked structure of large landowners, large farmers and a mass of landless labourers. It underwent rapid urbanisation, accompanied by the growing importance of non-landed social groups that consisted of people who gained their living primarily from manufacturing, trade and the provision of professional and other services. By 1750 the standards of living and material aspirations of most people had risen and this, together with a rapid increase in agricultural productivity and commercial expansion (especially in the century after 1650), produced expanding domestic and colonial markets that were one of the key elements in the promotion of rapid industrialisation in Britain from the later eighteenth century onwards. Parallel changes in ideas and attitudes – the growth of literacy, the influence of Protestantism and the emergence of an optimistic faith in reason and man's capacity to solve problems – are equally striking. In this process the period between 1650 and 1750 is at least as important as the previous century, which is often seen as an exceptional period of social change. It was not. The later seventeenth and early eighteenth centuries witnessed crucial changes in English society that amount, not to 'polarisation' either in a social or cultural sense, but to a departure from many (if not all) of the general characteristics of society elsewhere in Europe.

PART FIVE: DOCUMENTS

THE SOCIAL ORDER

Documents 1 and 2 reflect the ideal view of a fixed and ordered society that some legislators and commentators would have liked to see in early modern England. Document 3, which is one of the classic contemporary descriptions of the structure of early modern English society, indicates that in reality social mobility was common at this time. (See also Document 26.)

DOCUMENT 1 THE STATUTE OF ARTIFICERS (1563) CLAUSE 7

That none of the said reteyned persons in husbandrye or in eny the artes or sciences above remembered [these include all the major craft and manufacturing occupations] after the tyme of his reteynor expired, shall departe fourth of one citie towne or parishe to another, nor oute of the ... Hundred, nor oute of the Countie or Shire where he last served, to serve in any other Citie ... or Countie, unles he have a testymonyall under the Seale of the said Citie.

Tawney and Power [352], Vol. i, p. 341.

DOCUMENT 2 NATHANIEL CROUCH, *THE APPRENTICES COMPANION* (1681)

There is nothing more plain nor certain, than that God Almighty hath ordained and appointed degrees of Authority and Subjection, allowing Authority to the Master, and commanding obedience from the servant unto him; for God hath given express commands to Masters to govern their Servants, and to Servants to be subject to their Masters ... Christians in all Ages have asserted and owned this distinction, some of them having been placed as Masters and others as Servants, and according to the station which it hath pleased God to allot them, they have performed their mutual dutys.

R. W. Malcomson, *Life and Labour in England 1700–1780*, Hutchinson, 1981, p. 14.

DOCUMENT 3   **SIR THOMAS SMITH,** *DE REPUBLICA ANGLORUM* (1583)

Chapter 16. The divisions of the parts and persons of the Commonwealth.
We in England divide our men commonly into foure sortes, gentlemen, citizens or burgesses, yeomen artificers and laborers. Of gentlemen the first and chiefe be the king, the prince, dukes, marquises, earles, vicountes, and barrons, and this is called ... the nobility, and all these are called Lords and noblemen: next to these be knights, esquiers and simple gentlemen.

Chapter 17. Of the first part of gentlemen of England called nobilitas maior.
Dukes, marquises, erles, vicountes, and barrons, either be created of the prince or come to that honor by being the eldest sonnes, or highest in succession to their parentes ...

Chapter 18. Of the second sort of gentlemen which may be called nobilitas minor, *and first of knightes.*
No man is a Knight by succession ... Knightes therefore be not borne but made ... knightes in England are most commonly made according to the yearley revenew of their landes being able to maintain that estate ... [but] not all [are] made knightes in Englande that may spende a knightes landes but they onely whom the prince wil honour ...

Chapter 19. Of esquiers.
Escuie or esquier ... be all those which beare armes (as we call them) ... which to beare is a testimonie of the nobilitie or race from which they do come. These be taken for no distinct order of the common wealth, but do goe with the residue of the gentlemen

Chapter 20. Of gentlemen.
Gentlemen be those whom their blood and race doth make noble for that their ancestour hath bin notable in riches or for his vertues, or (in fewer words) old riches or prowes remaining in one stock. Which if the successors do keepe and follow, they be *vere nobiles* ... If they do not, the fame and riches of their auncestors serve to cover them so long as it can, as a thing once gilted though it be copper within, till the gilt be worn away ... as other common wealthes were faine to doe, so must all princes necessarilie followe, where vertue is to honour it ... the prince and common wealth have the same power that their predecessors had, and as the husbandman hath to plant a new tree when the olde fayleth, to honour vertue where he doth find it, to make gentlemen, esquiers knights, barons, earles, marquises, and dukes, where he seeth vertue able to bear that honour or merits, to deserve it, and so it hath always bin used among us. But ordinarily the king doth make knights and create the barons and higher degrees: for as gentlemen, they be made good cheape in England. For whosever studieth

the lawes of the realme, who studieth in the universities, who professeth liberall sciences, and to be shorte who can live idly and without manuall labour, and will bear the port, charge and countenaunce of a gentleman, he shall be called master, for that is the title which men give to esquires and other gentelmen, and shall be taken for a gentleman ... (and if neede be) a king of heralds shal also give him for money, armes newly made and invented, which the title shall beare that the said Herauld hath perused and seen old Registers where his auncestors in times past had borne the same ... These men be called sometime in scorne gentelmen of the first head.

Chapter 22. Of citizens and burgesses.
Next to a gentleman, be appointed citizens and burgesses, such as not onely be free and received as officers within the cities, but also be of some substance to beare the charges.

Chapter 23. Of yeomen.
Those whom we call yeomen next unto the nobilitie, the knights and squires, have the greatest charges and doings in the common wealth ... I call him a yeoman whom our lawes call *Legalem hominem* ... which is a freeman borne English, who may dispend of his own free lande in yerely revenue to the summe of xl.s sterling [£2] by the yeare ... This sort of people confesse themselves to be no gentleman, and yet they have a certaine preheminence and more estimation than labourers and artificers, and commonly live welthilie, keepe good houses, do their businesse, and travaile to get riches: they be (for the most part) fermours to gentlemen, and with grasing, frequenting of marquettes, and keeping servauntes, not idle servauntes as the gentlemen doth, but such as get their owne living and part of their maisters: by these meanes do come to such wealth, that they are able and daily doe buy the lands of unthriftie gentlemen, and after setting their sonnes to the schools, to the Universities, to the lawe of the Realme or otherwise leaving them sufficient landes wheron they may labour, doe make their said sonnes by these meanes gentlemen.

Chapter 24. Of the fourth sort of men which doe not rule.
The fourth sort or class amongest us is ... day labourers, poore husbandmen, yea merchantes or retailers which have no free lande, copiholders, all artificers, as Taylors, Shoomakers, Carpenters, Brickmakers, Bricklayers, Masons, &c. These have no voice nor authorities in our common wealth, and no account is made of these but onlie to be ruled, not to rule other, and yet they be not altogether neglected. For in cities and corporate townes for default of yeomen, they are faine to make their enquests of such manner of people. And in villages they be commonly made Churchwardens, alecunners, and manie times Constables ...

Smith [350], pp. 64–77.

AGRARIAN SOCIETY

Since England remained an agrarian society throughout the early modern
period, periodic failures of the harvest often had disastrous social
consequences, causing hunger and unemployment. It is not surprising,
therefore, that on such occasions, as in 1648, Ralph Josselin, the vicar of
Earl's Colne in Essex, devoted much space to this topic in his diary
(Document 4). But Document 5, written by a visitor from Brandenburg,
gives a more optimistic assessment of the state of English agriculture even in
the economically depressed 1590s and underlines the fact that people rarely
died of starvation even before 1650, after which agricultural productivity
improved dramatically.

DOCUMENT 4   RALPH JOSSELIN'S DIARY (1648)

May 1648. Among all the severall judgements on this nation, God this
spring, in the latter end of April, when rye was earing and eared, sent such
terrible frosts that the ear was frozen and so died.

June 1648. The Lord goeth out against us in the season, which was
wonderful wet, floods every week, hay rotted abroad. Much was carried
away with the floods, much inned but very dirty and dangerous for cattle.
Corn laid, pulled down with weeds. We never had the like in my memory,
and that for the greatest part of the summer.

Thirsk and Cooper [353], p. 49.

DOCUMENT 5   PAUL HENTZNER (1598)

The soil is fruitful and abounds with cattle, which inclines the inhabitants
rather to feeding than ploughing. So that near a third part of the land is left
uncultivated for grazing ... Though the soil is productive it bears no wine
... There are many hills without one tree or spring, which produce a very
short and tender grass, and supply plenty of food to sheep, upon these
wander numerous flocks extremely white, and whether from the
temperature of the air or the goodness of the earth, bearing softer and finer
fleeces than any other country. This is the true Golden Fleece in which
consists the chief riches of the inhabitants, great sums of money being
brought into the island by merchants, chiefly for that article of trade ...

W. B. Rye, ed., *England as seen by Foreigners in the Days of Elizabeth I*
and James I (1865), pp. 109–10.

CONTRASTING COMMUNITIES

John Aubrey's analysis of the county of Wiltshire is an extreme version of a common view held by people in early modern England that there were major differences (economic, social, religious and cultural) between 'forest' and 'fielden' types of communities. It is a distinction that has been used to good effect by modern social historians.

DOCUMENT 6   **JOHN AUBREY,** *THE NATURAL HISTORY OF WILTSHIRE*

In North Wiltshire, and like the vale of Gloucestershire (a dirty clayey country) the indigenae, or Aborigines, speake drawling; they are phlegmatique, skins pale and livid, slow and dull, heavy of spirit: herabout is but little tillage or hard labour, they only milk the cowes and make cheese; they feed chiefly on milke meates, which cooles their braines too much, and hurts their inventions. These circumstances make them melancholy, contemplatative and malicious; by consequence wherof come more law suites out of North Wilts, at least double to the Southern parts. And by the same reason they are generally more apt to be fanatiques ...

On the downes, sc. [*scilicet*=namely] the south part, where 'tis all upon tillage, and where the shepherds labour hard, their flesh is hard, their bodies strong: being weary after hard labour, they have not leisure to read and contemplate of religion, but goe to bed to their rest, to rise betime the next morning to their labour.

J. Aubrey, *The Natural History of Wiltshire ... Written between 1656 and 1691*, ed. John Britton (London 1847), p. 11.

FAMILY AND KINSHIP

Document 7 is a statement typical of many early modern commentators who recognised the centrality of the nuclear family in society, a fact which has recently been explored by historians. Students should be careful, however, not to take at face value all statements by contemporaries, like those in Document 8, about the patriarchal ordering of society. Documents 9 and 10 illustrate that relations within the early modern family were often more equal, warmer and closer than a reading of some contemporary treatises might suggest.

DOCUMENT 7   **SIR THOMAS SMITH,** *DE REPUBLICA ANGLORUM* (1583)

The naturalest and first conjunction of two towards the making of a further

societie of continuance is of the husband & of the wife ... And without this
societie of man, and woman, the kinde of man could not long endure.

Smith [350], p. 58.

DOCUMENT 8   **WILLIAM GOUGE,** *OF DOMESTICALL*
DUTIES *(1622)*

The husband is as a Priest unto his wife ... He is the highest in the family,
and hath authority over all and the charge of all is committed to his charge;
hee is as a king in his own house.

Davies [78], p. 566.

DOCUMENT 9   **SIR ANTHONY FITZHERBERT'S** *BOKE OF*
HUSBANDRY **(1523 AND SUBSEQUENTLY**
REPUBLISHED MANY TIMES IN THE
SIXTEENTH CENTURY)

It is a wives occupacion to winow al maner of comes, to make malte wash
and wring, to make hey, to shere corne, and in time of nede to helpe her
husbande to fyll the muck wayne or donge carte, dryve the plough, to lode
hey, corne & such other. Also to go or ride to the market to sell butter,
chese, mylke, egges, checkens, kapons, hennes, pygges, gees, and al maner
of come. And also to bye al maner of necessary thinges belonging to a
household, and to make a true rekening & accompt to her husband what
she hathe receyved and what she hathe payed. And yf the husband go to the
market to bye or sell as they ofte do, he then to shew his wife in lyke
maner. For if one of them should use to diseyveth him selfe, and he is not
lyke to thryve & therefore they must be true ether to other.

Clark [102], p. 49.

DOCUMENT 10   **ADAM MARTINDALE'S DIARY, 23 AUGUST**
1659, ON THE DEATH OF HIS EIGHT
YEAR OLD SON

I was gone to Chester when he died, my businesse being urgent, and he in a
hopefull way of recovery when I set out, (at least as we thought), and being
there I had an irresistible impression upon my spirit that I must needs go
home that night, (though I could not ghesse why, for I did not in the least
suspect his death) so that I left some considerable businesse undone which I

could have brought to an head the next day, and went home that evening, where I found a sad distracted family that needed much consolation and assistance from me; and I do verily believe that strong impression was from some angell that God employed to helpe on that worke.

Martindale [345], p. 109.

OTHER SOCIAL RELATIONSHIPS

The following four documents represent perceptions by contemporaries of different types of overlapping 'communities' that existed in early modern England outside the nuclear family. Neighbourhood ties were more important than those between wider kin for economic aid and work (Document 11), as well as for the enforcement of communal values by rituals like the skimmington in Wiltshire in 1618 (Document 12).

The election address of a Cheshire gentleman, Sir Richard Grosvenor, in 1624 (Document 13) reveals the dual attachment some people in this period felt for their own locality and the country at large. This accounts for the different meanings with which Grosvenor uses the word 'country'. He uses it first in a modern sense, referring to the national community; his second use of it refers to the local community of Cheshire.

Document 14 indicates the bond of patronage and good lordship (in this case between the landlord and his tenants on a Lancashire estate) that permeated all social relationships in early modern England.

DOCUMENT 11   **HENRY BEST'S FARMING BOOK (1641)**

It is usual in most places after they get all peas pulled or the last grain down, to invite all the workfolks and their wives (that helped them that harvest) to supper, and then they have puddings, bacon or boiled beef, flesh or apple pies, and then cream brought in platters, and everyone a spoon; then after all they have hot cakes and ale; for they bake cakes and send for ale against that time; some will cut their cake and put into the cream, and this feast is called the cream-pot or cream kitte; for on the morning that they get all done the workfolks will ask their dames if they have a good store of cream, and say they must have the cream kitte anon.

Thirsk and Cooper [353], pp. 125–6.

DOCUMENT 12   **WILTSHIRE QUARTER SESSIONS (TRINITY 1618)**

[Deposition of Thomas Mills, cutler, and his wife Agnes, of events that took place on 27 May 1618.]

... about noon came again from Caine to Quemerford another drummer named William Wiatt, and with him three or four hundred men, some like soldiers armed with pieces and other weapons, and a man riding upon a horse, having a white night cap upon his head, two shoeing horns hanging by his ears, a counterfeit beard upon his chin made of deer's tail, a smock upon the top of his garments, and he rode upon a real horse with a pair of pots under him, and in them some quantity of brewing grains, which he used to cast upon the press of people, rushing over thick upon him in the way as he passed; and he and all his company made a stand when they came just against this examinate's house, and then the gunners shot off their pieces, pipes and horns were sounded, together with lowbells and other similar bells which the company had amongest them, and rams' horns and bucks' horns, carried upon forks were then lifted up and shown. Thomas Mills ... locked the street door and locked his wife into his chamber where she lay ... and presentlie the parties abovementioned and divers others rushed in upon him into his entry, and thence into his hall, and broke open his chamber door upon his wife ... and ... took her up by the arms and the legs, and had her out through the hall into the entry, where being a wet hole, they threw her down into it and trod upon her and buried her filthily with dirt and did beat her black and blue in many places.

Ingram [135], p. 82, and W. Cunnington, ed., *Records of the County of Wiltshire*, (Devizes 1932), pp. 65–6.

DOCUMENT 13   **SIR RICHARD GROSVENOR'S ELECTION ADDRESS (1624)**

[Electors should vote for] those that are conversant in the affaires of the countrey and who thoroughlie understand the nature of this countie Palatine ... [M.P.s should] dare command their tongues, without fear to utter their countreyes just complaints and grievances, the waight of this ymployment is understood by taking a view of the nature of a parliament ... which is the highest court of the kingdom.

Cust and Lake [123], p. 45.

DOCUMENT 14   *THE MEMORANDA BOOK OF JAMES BANKES OF WINSTANLEY (1611)*

My deare children unto whom it shall pleas God to injoye this power houes of Wynstanley, I would advices you in Good most holye nam that you wold not in ane wyse deale harlye wyth ane tenant otherwyse then in this order and sort, that is to saye, I would have evere man to injoye his tenement dowring his les and his wyfes lyfe so after to his son if he have ane, and the les being ended I would have you ... to lett his son that is next unto it to make a les of the said farme ... and to be vere kynd and loving unto youre tenantes and so they wyll love you in good and godly sort.

J. Bankes and E. Kerridge, eds, *The Early Records of the Bankes Family at Winstanley*, (Chetham Society 1973), pp. 17–18.

POPULATION AND PRICE CHANGES

Document 15 is an overly gloomy assessment of the economic and social repercussions of the rise in population which began in England in the early sixteenth century and which lasted until the mid-seventeenth century; and Document 16 is too pessimistic about the effects of the subsequent period of population stagnation. But both suggest that some contemporaries were aware (as are modern historians) of important links between trends in population and prices and changes in the standard of living and the state of the economy.

DOCUMENT 15   **ROBERT GRAY,** *A GOOD SPEED TO VIRGINIA* **(1609)**

There is nothing more dangerous for the estate of commonwealths than when the people do increase to a greater multitude and number than may justly parallel with the largeness of the place and country. For hereupon comes oppression and diverse kinds of wrongs, mutinies, sedition, commotion, and rebellion, scarcity, dearth, poverty and sundry sorts of calamities ... Our multitudes, like too much blood in the body, do infect our country with plague and poverty. Our land hath brought forth but it hath not milk sufficient in the breast thereof to nourish all those children which it hath brought forth.

Thirsk and Cooper [353], pp. 757–8.

DOCUMENT 16   **CAREW REYNELL,** *THE TRUE ENGLISH INTEREST* **(1674)**

Of Marriage and Populacy. The country complains of small vend of commodities, which proceeds especially from want of people ... if we had but a million more of people than now, we should quickly see how trade and the vend of things would alter for the better. And this would hinder people from going out of the nation, when they may have found land, preferment, or employment here.

Thirsk and Cooper [353], pp. 758–9.

THE LAND-OWNING CLASSES

Document 3 includes the common contemporary definition of a 'gentleman' and of what distinguished land-owning gentlemen from 'the middling sort' immediately below them in landed society. But Smith's account, as does Document 17 which is taken from Wilson's description of the social order in 1600, recognises that the gulf between gentlemen and others could be (and was) crossed in this period. Indeed both the parvenu *who had recently become a gentleman and aspiring farmers were stock figures of fun in contemporary satirical and dramatic works (Documents 18 and 19). Complaints like those in Documents 20 and 21, that life at the top of landed society was not easy, smack of special pleading when seen in the context of the growing wealth and numbers of greater landowners in early modern England.*

DOCUMENT 17   **SIR THOMAS WILSON,** *THE STATE OF ENGLAND* **(1600)**

I know many yeomen in divers provinces in England which are able yearly to dispend betwixt three or five hundred pounds yearly by their lands and leases and some twice and some thrice as much; but my young masters the sons of such, not contented with the states of their fathers to be counted yeomen and called John or Robert (such an one), but must skip into his velvet breeches and silken doublet and, getting to be admitted into some Inn of Court or Chancery, must ever after think scorn to be called any other than gentleman.

Wilson [354], p. 19.

DOCUMENT 18   **RICHARD BROWNE,** *THE NORTHERN LASSE* **(1632), ACT 2 SCENE 1**

Widow: I'twere a cunning Herald could find better Arms for some of 'hem, though I have heard Sir Peter Squelch protest he was a Gentleman, and might quarto a Coat by his wives side. Yet I know he was but a Grazier when he left the Countrey; and my Lord his father whistled to a Team of Horses (they were his own indeed). But now he is Right Worshipfull.

Campbell [200], p. 45.

DOCUMENT 19   JOHN STEPHENS, *ESSAYES AND*
                CHARACTERS (1615)

A FARMER. To purchase arms (if he emulates gentry) sets upon him like
an ague: it breaks his sleep, takes away his stomach, and he can never be
quiet till the herald hath given him the harrows, the cuckoo, or some
ridiculous emblem for his armoury.

J. Dover Wilson, ed., *Life in Shakespeare's England*, (Penguin 1944), p. 31.

DOCUMENT 20   SEACOME, *MEMOIRS* ... *OF THE ANCIENT*
                AND HONOURABLE HOUSE OF STANLEY
                (1741)

[The Royalist James Stanley 7th earl of Derby was executed in 1651. His
son, the 8th earl] had scarce sufficient left to support the Honour and
Dignity of his character ... Insomuch that his eldest son and Successor Earl
William, whom I had the Honour to serve several Years as Household
Steward, hath often told me, that he possessed no Estate in Lancashire,
Cumberland, Westmorland, Yorkshire, Cheshire, Warwickshire and Wales;
but whenever he view'd any of them he cou'd see another near or adjoyning
to that he was in Posssession of equal, or greater of value lost by his
Grandfather for his Loyalty and service to the Crown and Country.

Coward [172], p. 76.

DOCUMENT 21   *AN ESSAY CONCERNING THE DECAY OF*
                RENTS ... *WRITTEN BY SIR WILLIAM*
                COVENTRY ABOUT THE YEAR 1670

That rents decay every landlord feels, the reasons and remedies are not so
well understood. Those which accrue to me as the most probable ground of
the fall of rents are: 1. Plenty of product. 2. Want of vent for our product.
3. Want of tenants. 4. Want of money to stock grounds and keep the
country markets.

Thirsk and Cooper [353], p. 79.

YEOMEN AND HUSBANDMEN

*Not all yeomen became landed gentlemen. Some, as well as smaller
husbandmen farmers, were forced off the land, a social change commented
on by Roger North, who probably wrote A* Discourse *in the first years of*

the eighteenth century (although published later, Document 22). The dictum of the leading legal theorist of the early seventeenth century (Document 23) is the one that has been used, convincingly, to show that the legal position of many early modern tenant farmers was more secure than many once thought. It seems likely that pressures arising from population changes, as John Norden's comment suggests (Document 24), were more important than legal considerations in determining the fate of many small farmers.

DOCUMENT 22   **ROGER NORTH,** *A DISCOURSE ON THE POOR* (1753)

It is another very great Destruction of People, as well as Impediment to the Recruit of them, that Gentlemen, of late Years, have taken up an Humour of destroying their Tenements and Cottages, whereby they make it impossible that mankind should inhabit their Estates. This is done sometimes bare-faced ... they cast their Lands into very great Farms, which are managed with less Housing; and oftimes for Improvement, as it is called; which is done by buying in all Freeholds, Copyholds, and Tenements that have Commons, and which harboured very many husbandry and labouring Families; and then enclosing the Commons and Fields, turning the managing from Tillage to Grazing.

DOCUMENT 23   **SIR EDWARD COKE,** *THE COMPLETE COPYHOLDER* (1641)

In respect of the state of the land, so copyholders may be freeholders; for any that hath any estate in any lands whatsoever, may in this sense be termed a freeholder.

Kerridge [202], p. 164.

DOCUMENT 24   **JOHN NORDEN,** *THE SURVEYOR'S DIALOGUE* (1607), *p. 15*

I have seen and observed among them [tenant farmers] a kind of madnesse. When the Lord hath beene at liberty to dispose therof [i.e. to let some of his estates] at his will, for best advantage by choyse of a new Tenant, proclamation to that effect hath beene made in open Court, where I have seene, and it is daily in use, that one will out-bid another, in so much I have wondered at their emulation.

John Norden *The Surveyor's Dialogue* (1607), p. 15.

LABOURERS, SERVANTS AND VAGRANTS

Descriptions of the lives of labourers and servants were usually written by wealthy people who either knew little or were unsympathetic about their plight. Smith (Document 3) comes into the former category and Defoe (Document 25) the latter. Defoe's hostile comment on the alleged idleness of labourers and servants, although typical of the attitudes throughout the early modern period of the rich towards those they considered to be their inferiors, was especially widely-held in the century after 1650, when wage rates of labourers were rising. Information about vagrants, too, often comes from hostile commentators, who described bands of sturdy beggars wandering the country as a 'many-headed monster', a threat to property (Document 31). In reality, as Document 26 illustrates, the lives of most vagrants were pathetic and represented no real threat to the existing social order.

DOCUMENT 25   **DANIEL DEFOE,** *THE TRUE-BORN ENGLISHMAN: A SATIRE* (1701)

> The Lab'ring poor, in spite of double pay,
> Are saucy, mutinous and beggarly;
> So lavish of their money and their time,
> That want of forecast is the nation's crime.
> Good drunken company is their delight;
> And what they get by day they spend by night.
> Dull thinking seldom does their heads engage,
> But drink their youth away, and hurry on old age.

D. Defoe, *The Novels and Miscellaneous Works*, (Bohn's Standard Library 1905), p. 444.

DOCUMENT 26   **CERTIFICATE OF 'VAGABONDES, ROGUES AND MIGHTY VALIAUNT BEGGARS', TAKEN BY NICHOLAS POWTRELL, JP, AT SOUTHCLEY, NOTTS., 20 AUGUST 1571**

2,3,4. Isabell Cotton, Anne Draper, John Draper taken at Normanton as vagrant persons, examined, whipped and punnished and after sent from Constable to Constable the direct waie to Bolton in Lancashier where they were borne and dwell.
5. Jennet Johnson taken at Normanton as a vagarant person, examined, whipped, stocked and punnished and after sent from Constable to

Constable the direct waie to Tolton in the Countie of York, where he last dwelled the space of three yeares and more.

Tawney and Power [352], Vol. ii, p. 327.

CRAFTSMEN AND TRADESMEN

Despite the hopes some people had of preventing major social changes taking place (Documents 1 and 2), by the later seventeenth and early eighteenth centuries the number of workers whose lives were completely divorced from the land had increased, a fact reflected in the journals of the two most famous travellers in later Stuart and early Hanoverian England, Celia Fiennes (Document 27) and Daniel Defoe (Document 28).

DOCUMENT 27   CELIA FIENNES, THE NORTHERN JOURNEY AND TOUR OF KENT (1697)

[At Nottingham] they make brick and tile by the town; the manufacture of the town mostly consists in weaving of Stockings, which is a very ingenious art; there was a man that spunn Glass and made severall things in Glass birds and beasts, I spunn some of the glass and saw him make a Swan presently, with divers colloured glass he makes Buttons which are very strong and will not breake; Nottingham is very famous for good ale.

C. Morris, ed., *The Illustrated Journeys of Celia Fiennes 1685–c.1712*, (Macdonald 1982), p. 88.

DOCUMENT 28   DANIEL DEFOE, A TOUR THROUGH ENGLAND AND WALES (1723)

When we came into Norfolk, we see a face of diligence spread over the whole country; the vast manufacturers carry'd on (in chief) by Norwich weavers, employs all the country round in spinning yarns for them; besides many thousand packs of yarn which they receive from all other countries, even as far as Yorkshire and Westmorland ... An eminent weaver of Norwich gave me a scheme of their trade on this occasion, by which, calculating from the number of looms at the time employ'd in other towns in the same county he made it appear very plain, that there were 120,000 people employ'd in the woollen and silk and wool manufactures of that city only, not that the people all lived in the city ... This shews the wonderful extent of the Norwich manufacture, or stuff-weaving trade, by which so many thousands of families are maintained ... as I pass'd this part of the country in the year 1723, the manufacturers assured me, that there was not in all the eastern and middle of Norfolk, any hand, unemploy'd, if they could work ... If a stranger was only to ride thro' or view the city of Norwich for a day, he would have more reason to think there was a town without inhabitants ... but on the contrary, if he was to view the city, either on a sabbathday, or any public occasion, he would wonder where all the people could dwell, the multitude is so great: But the case is this; the inhabitants being all busie at their manufactures dwell in their garrets at their looms, and in their combing shops, so they call them, twisting mills, and other work-houses; almost all the works, they are employ'd in, being done within doors.

D. Defoe, *A Tour through the Whole Island of Great Britain* (1726), (Everyman 1962), Vol. i, pp. 61–3.

PROFESSIONALS AND 'THE MONIED INTEREST'

All contemporary analyses of social changes in early modern England should be looked at with a great deal of scepticism and the following two documents are no exception. John Aubrey (Document 29) reflects a hostility to lawyers that is by no means typical only of the seventeenth century, and Henry St John's fears of the growth of 'the monied interest' at the expense of 'the landed interest' (Document 30) were grossly exaggerated for reasons that lie in the bitter party political rivalries of the reign of Queen Anne. Yet both comments at least indicate the fact, if not the scale, of the growing importance in early modern English society of people whose wealth was not primarily derived from land.

DOCUMENT 29   **JOHN AUBREY,** *THE NATURAL HISTORY OF WILTSHIRE ... WRITTEN BETWEEN 1656 AND 1691*

Mr Baynham of Cold Aston in Gloucestershire, bred an attorney, says that an hundred years since there were in the county of Gloucester but four attorneys and solicitors; and Dr Godot, physician, of Bath, says that they report that anciently there was but one attorney in Somerset, and he was so poor that he went afoot to London; and now they swarm like locust ... Fabian Philips tells me (1683) that about sixty nine years ago there were but two attorneys in Worcestershire, sc. Langston and Dowdeswell; and they be now in every market town, and go to market and he believes there are a hundred ... 'tis thought in England there are at this time near three thousand (attorneys).

Holmes [225], p. 151.

DOCUMENT 30   HENRY ST JOHN'S LETTER TO LORD
ORRERY (JULY 1709)

We have now been twenty years engaged in the two most expensive warrs
that Europe ever saw. The whole burthen of this charge has lain upon the
landed interest during the whole time. The men of estates have, generally
speaking, neither served in the fleets nor armies, nor meddled in the public
funds & management of the treasure.

A new interest has been created out of their fortunes, & a sort of
property wch was not known twenty years ago is now encreased to almost
equal to the terra firma of our island. The consequence of all this is that the
landed men are become poor & dispirited, They either abandon all thoughts
of the publick, turn arrant farmers & improve their estates they have left; or
else they seek to repair their shattered fortunes by listing at Court, or under
the head of Partys. In the mean while those men are become their masters,
who formerly with joy would have been their servants.

Holmes [223], p. 177.

POVERTY AND DEARTH

*The great extent of poverty in early modern England aroused diverse
reactions from contemporaries. Document 31 by a Somerset JP is typical of
those who reacted with horror to it and feared that, unless the poor were
savagely repressed, they would attack and overturn the existing social order.
Others, however, realised that not all the poor were shiftless people to be
punished; some were poor because of circumstances beyond their control
and should be protected. William Harrison's view (Document 32) reflects
the kind of thinking that resulted in public and private schemes of poor
relief for the deserving poor begun in the late sixteenth century when the
population was rising rapidly. When the demographic pressure eased after
1650, so the fears of people like Hext diminished. The poor came to be seen
(not only by reformers like Goffe in the mid-seventeenth century, Document
33) not as a threat but as an asset that could be used to bring about
national economic growth.*

DOCUMENT 31   EDWARD HEXT'S LETTER TO LORD
BURGHLEY (1596)

For god ys my wiytnesse I do with grief protest yn the dewtye of a subiecte,
I do not see howe yt ys possible for the poore Cuntryman to beare the
burthens dewly layde uppon hym, and the rapynes of the Infynytt numbers

of the wicked wandrynge Idell people of the land. So as men are dryven to watch ther sheepefolds, ther pastures, ther woods, ther Cornfylds, all things growing too too [*sic*] comon. Others there be (and I feare me imboldened by the wandrynge people) that styck not to say boldlye they must not starve, they will not starve ... which may grow dangerous by the ayde of suche numbers as are abroade, especyally in this tyme of dearthe, who no dowpt anymate them to all contempte bothe of noble men and gentlemen, contynially Bussynge into there eares that the ritche men have gotten all into ther hands and will starve the poor. And I may lustlie say that the Infynyte numbers of the Idle wandrynge people and robbers of the land are the chefest cause of the dearthe, for thowghe they labor not, and yet they spend dobly as myche as the laborer dothe, for they lye idely in the ale howses daye and nygh eatinge and drynkinge excessively.

Tawney and Power [352], Vol. ii, pp. 341–2.

DOCUMENT 32   **WILLIAM HARRISON,** *DESCRIPTION OF ENGLAND* **(1587)**

With us the poor is commonly divided into three Sorts, so that some are poor by impotency, as the fatherless child, the aged, blind and lame, and the diseased person that is judged to be incurable: the second are poor by casualty, as the wounded soldier, the decayed householder, and the sick person visited with grievous and painful diseases: the third consisteth of thriftless poor, as the rioter that hath consumed all, the vagabond that will abide nowhere but runneth up and down from place to place, and finally the rogue and the strumpet.

Harrison [339], p. 180.

DOCUMENT 33   **WILLIAM GOFFE,** *HOW TO ADVANCE THE TRADE OF THE NATION AND EMPLOY THE POOR* **(C.1650)**

The poor ought to be encouraged and mercifully dealt with and kindly used, until slow hands be brought to ready working and ought at first to have the highest price the commodity will bear to themselves.

T. F. Gregory, 'The economics of employment in England 1660–1713', *Economica* 1, (1921–2), p. 50.

URBAN SOCIETY

In the later sixteenth and early seventeenth centuries rich influential opinion reacted to the growth of London in much the same way as Hext reacted to the poor: with horror. The growth of London was seen as a potential source of disorder and the cause of the decline of provincial towns (Document 34). This view gained support because before 1650 London's rapid growth was not matched by provincial towns. However, by the later seventeenth and early eighteenth centuries it became much more common to emphasise (as does Defoe in Document 35) the positive aspects of London as 'an engine of economic growth', largely because in this period it was now apparent that London's growth was merely part of the vitality of English urban life as a whole. (See also Documents 27 and 28.)

DOCUMENT 34   **A LETTER TO THE MASTER OF THE ROLLS (1590)**

Wheras yt pleased the Queen's Majestie more than two yeres past to comand proclamacion to be published for the restrayning and prohibiting of new building of houses and tenements for habitacon in and about the Citie of London, whereby as by the acces of multitudes of people to inhabit the same and the perstering of many families in ine smale house or tenemente termed inmats and undersitters, the Citie hath been over largelie increased to the decaie of other townes, buroughes and villages within the Realme.

Tawney and Power [352], Vol. i, pp. 130–1.

DOCUMENT 35   **DANIEL DEFOE, *A TOUR THROUGH ENGLAND AND WALES* (1723)**

This whole kingdom, as well the people, as the land and even the sea, in every part of it, are employ'd to furnish something, and I may add, the best of every thing, to supply the city of London with provisions; I mean by provisions, corn, flesh, fish, butter, cheese, salt, fuel, timber etc. and cloths also; with every thing necessary for building, and furniture for their own use, or for trades.

D. Defoe, *A Tour through the Whole Island of Great Britain* (1724–6), (Everyman 1962), Vol. i, p. 12.

A CONSUMER SOCIETY

During the later seventeenth and early eighteenth centuries many contemporaries commented on the growing numbers of people who could afford goods previously only bought by the rich. Not everyone did so approvingly, and some, like Henry Fielding, saw the trend as the source of many contemporary social evils (Document 36). But other influential writers, like Bernard Mandeville (Document 37), saw growing demand for consumer goods as the mainspring of England's economic revitalisation. That there was a lively demand for consumer goods is suggested by the Quaker William Stout's account of his life as a shopkeeper in Lancaster in the later seventeenth century.

DOCUMENT 36   HENRY FIELDING, *ENQUIRY INTO THE CAUSES OF THE LATE INCREASE OF ROBBERS* (1750)

Nothing has wrought such an alteration in the order of people, as the introduction of trade. This hath indeed given a new face to the whole nation, hath in great measure subverted the former state of affairs, and hath almost totally changed the manners, customs and habits of the people, more especially the lower sort. The narrowness of their future is changed into wealth, their frugality into luxury, their humility into pride, and their subjection into equality.

McKendrick [284], p. 24.

DOCUMENT 37   BERNARD MANDEVILLE, *THE FABLE OF THE BEES* (1714)

Luxury
Employ'd a Million of the Poor,
And Odious Pride a Million More.
Envy it self, and Vanity
Were Ministers of Industry,
Their darling Folly, Fickleness
In Diet, Furniture and Dress,
That strange ridic'lous Vice, was made
The very wheel that turn'd their Trade

Thus Vice nursed Ingenuity,
Which join'd with Time, and Industry
Had Carry'd Life's Conveniences,
Its real Pleasures, Comforts, Ease,
To such a height, the very Poor
Lived better than the Rich before.

McKendrick [284], p. 17.

DOCUMENT 38   *THE AUTOBIOGRAPHY OF WILLIAM*
               STOUT (1682)

I was mostly imployed in the shop in the weekdays, in making up goods for
the market day, as sugar, tobbacco, nayls and other goods, and particularly
prunes, which we made up in the summer time about one hundred weight
weekly in pounds and two pounds ... and brandy ... tobbacco 2d [1p] a
pound, retailed at 6d [2½p], which causes a great consumption; and three
or four of us fully imployed every market day in delivering out goods, so
that we had a full trade then, and the best of customers.

Stout [351], pp. 79–80.

EDUCATION AND LITERACY

The growth of Protestantism in the later sixteenth and early seventeenth
centuries generally encouraged the development of educational opportunities
and the spread of literacy. For some conventionally minded Protestants, like
the Duke of Newcastle (Document 39), however, the events of the 1640s
and 1650s caused them to wonder whether encouraging ordinary people to
read had been such a good idea, and his prescription for the maintenance of
social order in the future was a programme of educational 'cuts'. It is
uncertain how effective such sentiments were in retarding the expansion of
educational opportunities in the later seventeenth and early eighteenth
centuries. What is certain is that circumstantial evidence, including
autobiographies (like that written by Thomas Tryon, who was born in 1634
the son of a poor Oxfordshire tiler and plasterer, Document 40) and other
occasional references (like Pepys's observation in 1667, Document 41)
suggest that not all ordinary people were illiterate and cut off from the
learned culture of the day.

DOCUMENT 39   **THE DUKE OF NEWCASTLE'S ADVICE TO**
               CHARLES II (1660)

The Bible in English under every weaver's and chambermaid's arms hath
done us much hurt. That which made it one way is the universities.
Abounds with too many scholars. Therefore, if every college had but half
the number, they would be better fed and as well taught. But that which
hath done us most hurt is the abundance of grammar schools and inns of
court ... And there are so many schools now as most read. So indeed there
should be, but such a proportion as to serve the church and moderately the
law and the merchants, and the rest for the labour, for else they run out to

idle and unnecessary people that becomes a factious burthen to the Commonwealth. For when most was unlettered, it was much a better world both for peace and war.

J. Thirsk, ed., *The Restoration*, (Longman 1976), pp. 170–1.

DOCUMENT 40   **THOMAS TRYON,** *SOME MEMOIRS OF THE LIFE OF MR THO. TRYON, LATE OF LONDON, MERCHANT: WRITTEN BY HIMSELF ...* (1705)

About five years old, I was put to School, but being addicted to play, after the Example of my young School-fellows, I scarcely learnt to distinguish my Letters before I was taken away to work for my Living [spinning and carding wool – subsequently he became a shepherd.] All this while, tho' now about Thirteen Years Old, I could not read; then thinking of the vast usefulness of Reading, I bought me a Primer, and got now one, then another, to teach me to Spell, and so learned to Read imperfectly, my Teachers themselves not being ready Readers. But in a little time having learn't to Read competently well, I was desirous to learn to Write, but was at a great loss for a Master, none of my Fellow-Shepherds being able to teach me. At last I bethought myself of a lame young Man who taught some poor People's Children to Read and Write; and having by this time got two Sheep of my own, I applied myself to him, and agreed with him to give him one of my Sheep to teach me to make the Letters, and Joyn them together.

Spufford [303], pp. 415–16.

DOCUMENT 41   **SAMUEL PEPYS'S DIARY, 14 JULY 1667, ON A VISIT TO EPSOM**

We found a shepherd and his little boy reading, far from any houses or sight of people, the Bible to him.

Pepys [347], Vol. viii, p. 338.

THE IMPACT OF PROTESTANTISM

The most famous (and vocal) products of the impact of Protestantism on English society in the later sixteenth and early seventeenth centuries are the Puritans. What is not often realised is that they shared many of the central beliefs of mainstream English Protestants. Nevertheless, as the auto-biographies of Puritans like Richard Baxter (Document 42) indicate, they felt themselves and were felt by other Protestants to be different and set apart by their distinctive life-styles. Yet they were a minority in English society and their attempts to impose a Puritan 'reformation of manners' in the 1640s met hostile resistance, typified by the conservative demands of those, like the Clubmen in Sussex, who wanted a restoration of the Elizabethan Church based on the Book of Common Prayer (Document 43). Such opposition became even more intense when the relative religious freedom of the 1640s and 1650s led to the excesses of a 'seeker' like Lawrence Clarkson (Document 44). In these circumstances the militant intolerance of the Clarendon Code at the Restoration, of which the Act of Uniformity is a part (Document 45), comes as no surprise.

DOCUMENT 42   THE AUTOBIOGRAPHY OF RICHARD BAXTER

In the village [Eaton Constantine in Shropshire] where I lived [as a teenager in the 1620s] the reader read the Common Prayer briefly, and the rest of the day even till dark night almost, except eating time, was spent in dancing under a maypole, and a great tree not far from my father's door, where all the town did meet together ... So that we could not read the Scripture in our family without the great disturbance of the tabor and pipe and noise in the street. Many times my mind was inclined to be among them, and sometimes I broke loose from conscience and joined with them, and the more I did it the more was I inclined to it. But when I heard them call my father Puritan it did much to cure me and alienate me from them: for I considered that my father's exercise of reading the Scripture was better than theirs, and would surely be thought on by all men at the last; and I considered what it was for that he and others were thus derided.

Baxter [334], p. 6.

DOCUMENT 43   THE PETITION OF THE SUSSEX CLUBMEN, 26 SEPTEMBER 1645

Imprimis the want of Church government whereby our Churches are decayed, God's ordinances neglected, orthodox Ministers cast out without cause and never heard, Mechanickes and unknowne persons thrust in, whoe were never called as Aaron but by Committeemen, whereby God and the Parliament are dishonoured and the people grieved.

J. Morrill, *The Revolt of the Provinces*, (Longman 1980), p. 198.

DOCUMENT 44   LAWRENCE CLARKSON, *THE LOST SHEEP FOUND (CLARKSON'S AUTOBIOGRAPHY)* (1660)

After the start of the Civil War Clarkson's dislike of the Church of England as it had developed in the 1630s led him to sample various kinds of religious beliefs, becoming a Presbyterian, then an Independent and subsequently a Baptist. Eventually he became a Ranter.

Now observe at this time my Judgment was this, that there was no man could be free'd from sin, till he had acted that so called sin, as no sin, this a certain time had been burning within me, yet durst not reveal it to any. [He began to try to convince others of the truth of this libertine philosophy with some success, as on one occasion] I pleaded the words of Paul, *That I know and am persuaded by the Lord Jesus, that there was nothing unclean, but as man esteemed it*, unfolding that was intended all acts, as well as meats and drinks, and therefore till you can lie with all women as one woman, and not judge it sin, you can do nothing but sin: now in Scripture I found a perfection spoken of; so that I understood no man could attain perfection but this way, at which Mr. Rawlinson was much taken, and Sarah Kullin, being then present, did invite me to make trial of what I had expressed, so as I take it, after we parted she invited me to Mr. Wats in Rood Lane, where was one or two more like herself; and as I take it, lay with me that night ...

L. Clarkson, *The Lost Sheep Found*, (University of Exeter 1974), pp 25–6.

DOCUMENT 45   **THE ACT OF UNIFORMITY (1662)**

Wheras in the first year of the late Queen Elizabeth there was one uniform Order of Common Service and prayer and of the administration of Sacraments, Rites and ceremonies in the Church of England (agreeable to the Word of God and usage of the Primitive Church) compiled by the reverend Bishops and clergy, set forth in one book, entitled 'The Book of Common Prayer' ... and wheras by the great and scandalous neglect of ministers in using the said order of liturgy so set forth and enjoined as aforesaid great mischiefs and inconveniences during the times of the late unhappy troubles have arisen and grown, and many people have been led into factions and schisms, to the great decay and scandal of the reformed religion of the Church of England, and to the hazard of many souls ...

J. P. Kenyon, ed., *The Stuart Constitution*, 2nd edn (Cambridge University Press 1986), p. 353.

THE SCIENTIFIC REVOLUTION

The optimism inherent in the new science, that became increasingly influential in many aspects of English society during the course of the seventeenth century, is neatly captured in the extract from Bacon's works (Document 46). Like other social trends in the early modern period, however, scientific rationalism did not triumph totally. Intellectual scepticism voiced by writers like Meric Causabon is reflected in one of the most famous pieces of popular literature written in the early eighteenth century, Gulliver's Travels (Document 47). In this extract from 'A Voyage to Laputa' in which Gulliver is shown the Grand Academy of Lagado, Swift savagely satirises the gulf between the aims and achievements of the Royal Society.

DOCUMENT 46   **SIR FRANCIS BACON, *NOVUM ORGANUM* (1620)**

Now the true and lawful goal of the sciences is none other than this: that human life is endowed with new discoveries and powers ... So much then for removing of despair and the raising of hope through the dismissal or rectification of the error of past time. We must now see what else there is to ground hope upon. And this consideration occurs at once – that if many useful discoveries have been made by accident or upon occasion, when men were not seeking for them but were busy about other things; no one can doubt but that when they apply themselves to seek and make this their business, and that too by method and in order and not by desultory impulses, they will discover far more ... far better things and more of them, and at shorter intervals, are to be expected from man's reason and industry and direction and fixed application than from accident and animal instinct and the like, in which inventions have hitherto had their origin.

J. M. Robertson, ed., *The Philosophical Works of Francis Bacon*, (1905), pp. 280, 291.

DOCUMENT 47   **JONATHAN SWIFT, *GULLIVER'S TRAVELS* (1726)**

I was received very kindly by the Warden and went for many Days to the Academy. Every Room hath in it one or more Projectors; and I believe I could not be in fewer than five Hundred Rooms ... The first Man I saw was of meagre Aspect, with sooty Hands and Face, his Hair and Beard long, ragged and singed in several Places. His Clothes, Shirt and Skin were all of the same Colour. He had been Eight Years upon a Project for extracting Sun-Beams out of Cucumbers, which were to be put into Viles hermetically sealed, and let out to warm the air in raw inclement Summers ... There was a most ingenious Architect who had contrived a new Method for building Houses, by beginning at the Roof; and working downwards to the Foundation ... In another Apartment I was highly pleased with a Projector, who had found a Device of plowing the Ground with Hogs, to save the Charges of Plows, Cattle, and Labour. The Method is this: in an Acre of ground you bury at six Inches Distance, and eight deep a Quantity of Acorns, Dates, Chesnuts, and other Masts or Vegetables wherof these Animals are fondest; then you drive six Hundred or more of them into the Field, where in a few Days they will root up the whole Ground in search of their Food, and make it fit for sowing, at the same time manuring it with their Dung. It is true, upon Experiment they found the Charge and the Trouble very great, and they had little or no Crop. However, it is not doubted that this Invention may be capable of great Improvement.

Swift, *Gulliver's Travels*, (Collins 1953), pp. 197–9.

BIBLIOGRAPHY

Note: the following abbreviations are used: *Econ. H. R.* (*Economic History Review*, 2nd series); *P. & P.* (*Past and Present*); and *T. R. H. S.* (*Transactions of the Royal Historical Society*, 5th series). The bibliography begins with a list of nine general books. The rest of the bibliography is divided into sections that are based on the chapters of the book. In each section the best introductory books and articles to the relevant topics are indicated by an asterisk*.

GENERAL SURVEYS:

The best one-volume introduction to the social history of the whole period is:

1* J. A. Sharpe, *Early Modern England: a Social History 1550–1760*, Arnold, 1987.

Nos 2 and 3 are good starting-points for (respectively) the earlier and later parts of the period.

2* D. Palliser, *The Age of Elizabeth*, 2nd edn, Longman, 1983.
3* K. Wrightson, *English Society 1580–1680*, Hutchinson, 1982.

Other useful general surveys are:

4   C. G. A. Clay, *Economic Expansion and Social Change in England 1500–1700*, 2 vols. Cambridge University Press, 1984.
5   P. Langford, *A Polite and Commercial People: England 1727–83*, Clarendon Press, 1989.
6   P. Laslett, *The World We Have Lost Further Explored*, 3rd edn., Methuen, 1983.
7   R. Porter, *English Society in the Eighteenth Century*, Penguin, 1982.
8   J. Rule, *Albion's People: English Society in the Eighteenth Century 1714–1815*, Longman, 1992.
9   J. Youings, *Sixteenth-Century England*, Harmondsworth, 1984.

THE SOCIAL ORDER IN EARLY MODERN ENGLAND:

10 J. Barry and C. Brooks (eds), *The Middling Sort of People*, Macmillan, 1994.

11 J. C. D. Clark, *English Society 1688–1832: Ideology, Society, Social Structure and Political Practice during the Ancien Regime*, Cambridge University Press, 1985.

12 P. Corfield, 'Class by name and number in eighteenth-century England', *History*, 72, 1987. Revised in P. Corfield (ed.), *Language, History and Class*, Oxford, 1991.

13* D. Cressy, 'Describing the social order of Elizabethan and early Stuart England', *Literature and History*, 3, 1976.

14 A. Everitt, 'Social mobility in early modern England', *P. & P.*, no. 33, 1966.

15 A. Everitt, Change in the Provinces: the Seventeenth Century (Leicester University Department of English Local History, occasional papers, 2nd series, vol. i, 1969).

16 N. B. Harte, 'State control of dress and social change in pre-industrial England', in D. C. Coleman and A. H. John (eds), *Trade, Government and Economy in Pre-industrial England*, Weidenfeld, 1976.

17 J. H. Hexter, 'The myth of the middle class in Tudor England', in his *Reappraisals in History*, Longman, 1961.

18 G. Holmes, 'Gregory King and the social structure of pre-industrial England', *T. R. H. S.*, 27, 1977.

19 A. Macfarlane, *The Origins of English Individualism*, Blackwell, 1978.

20 R. S. Schofield, 'The geographical distribution of wealth in England 1334–1649', *Econ. H. R.*, 18, 1965.

21 J. Thirsk, 'Seventeenth-century agriculture and social change', in J. Thirsk (ed.), *Land, Church and People*, British Agricultural History Society, 1970.

22 E. P. Thompson, 'Eighteenth-century society: class struggle without class?', *Social History*, 3, 1978.

23 E. M. W. Tillyard, *The Elizabethan World Picture*, Chatto and Windus, 1943.

24* K. Wrightson, 'The social order of early modern England: three approaches' in L. Bonfield, *et al.* (eds), *The World We Have Gained: Histories of Population and Social Structure*, Oxford, 1980.

GEOGRAPHICAL MOBILITY:

25* P. Clark, 'The migrant in Kentish towns 1558–1640', in 265.

26* P. Clark, 'Migration in England during the later seventeenth and early eighteenth centuries', *P. & P.*, no. 83, 1979.

27 D. Souden, 'Indentured servant emigrants to north America: the case of Bristol', *Social History*, 3, 1978.

THE AGRARIAN ECONOMY: THE ECONOMIC BACKGROUND:

28 M. Berg, *The Age of Manufacturers 1700–1820*, Routledge, 1985.
29 D. Cannadine, 'The past and present in the English Industrial Revolution 1880–1980', *P. & P.*, no 103, 1984.
30 J. A. Chartres, *Internal Trade in England 1500–1700*, Macmillan, 1977.
31 L. A. Clarkson, 'The leather crafts in Tudor and Stuart England', *Agricultural History Review*, 14, 1960.
32 D. C. Coleman, *Industry in Tudor and Stuart England*, Macmillan, 1975.
33* D. C. Coleman, *The Economy of England 1450–1750*, Oxford University Press, 1977.
34 R. Davis, *English Overseas Trade 1500–1700*, Macmillan, 1973.
35 C. J. Harrison, 'Grain price analysis and harvest qualities 1465–1634', *Agricultural History Review*, 19, 1971.
36 M. A. Havinden, 'Agricultural progress in open-field Oxfordshire', *Agricultural History Review*, 9, 1961.
37 B. A. Holderness, 'Credit in English rural society before the nineteenth century', *Agricultural History Review*, 29, 1976.
38 W. G. Hoskins, 'Harvest fluctuations and English economic history 1480–1759', *Agricultural History Review*, 12, 1964 and 16, 1968.
39 E. L. Jones (ed.), *Agriculture and Economic Growth in England 1650–1815*, Methuen 1967.
40 E. Kerridge, *The Agricultural Revolution*, Allen and Unwin, 1967.
41 M. Overton, *Agricultural Revolution in England: The Transformation of the Agrarian Economy 1500–1850*, Cambridge University Press, 1996.
42 J. Thirsk, 'Industries in the countryside', in F. J. Fisher (ed.), *Essays in the Economic and Social History of Tudor and Stuart England*, Cambridge University Press, 1961.
43 J. Thirsk (ed.), *The Agrarian History of England and Wales, iv, 1500–1640*, Cambridge University Press, 1967.
44 J. Thirsk (ed.), *The Agrarian History of England and Wales, v, 1640–1750*, 2 parts, Cambridge University Press, 1985.
45 T. S. Willan, *The Inland Trade: Studies in English Internal Trade in the Sixteenth and Seventeenth Centuries*, Manchester University Press, 1976.
46 C. Wilson, *England's Apprenticeship 1603–1763*, 2nd edn, Longman, 1985.

LOCAL STUDIES OF RURAL ENGLAND: CONTRASTING COMMUNITIES:

47 A. B. Appleby, 'Agrarian capitalism or seigneurial reaction? The north-west of England 1600–1700', *American Historical Review*, 80, 1975.

48   J. H. Bettey, *Wessex from AD 1000: A Regional History of England*, Longman, 1986.

49   J. D. Chambers, *Nottinghamshire in the Eighteenth Century*, P. S. King, 1932.

50   A. C. Chibnall, *Sherington: Fiefs and Fields of a Buckinghamshire Village*, Cambridge University Press, 1965.

51   P. Frost, 'Yeomen and metalsmiths: livestock in the dual economy in south Staffordshire, 1560–1720', *Agricultural History Review*, 29, 1981.

52   D. Hey, *An English Rural Community: Myddle under the Tudors and Stuarts*, Leicester University Press, 1974.

53   D. Hey, 'A dual economy in south Yorkshire', *Agricultural History Review*, xvii, 1969.

54   B. A. Holderness, ' "Open" and "closed" parishes in England in the eighteenth and nineteenth centuries', *Agricultural History Review*, 20, 1972.

55   J. P. Horn, 'The distribution of wealth in the Vale of Berkeley in Gloucestershire 1660–1700', *Southern History*, 3, 1980.

56   W. G. Hoskins, *The Midland Peasant: The Economic and Social History of a Leicestershire Village*, Macmillan, 1957.

57   C. Howell, *Land, Family and Inheritance in Transition: Kibworth Harcourt 1280–1700*, Cambridge University Press, 1983.

58   C. Husbands, 'Standards of living in north Warwickshire in the seventeenth century', *Warwickshire History*, 4, 1981.

59   R. E. Jones, 'Population and agrarian change in an eighteenth-century Shropshire parish', *Local Population Studies*, 1, 1968.

60   E. Kerridge, 'Agriculture c.1500–c.1793', in *Victoria County History of Wiltshire*, 4, 1959.

61   M. K. McIntosh, *A Community Transformed: The Manor and Liberty of Havering 1500–1620*, Cambridge University Press, 1991.

62   J. D. Marshall, 'Agrarian wealth and social structure in pre-industrial Cumbria', *Econ. H. R.*, 33, 1980.

63   P. A. J. Pettit, *The Royal Forests of Northamptonshire*, Northants Record Society, 1968.

64   M. B. Rowlands, *Masters and Men in the West Midlands Metalware Trades*, Manchester University Press, 1975.

65   V. Skipp, 'Economic and social change in the Forest of Arden 1530–1649', in J. Thirsk (ed.), *Land, Church and People*, British Agricultural History Society, 1970.

66   V. Skipp, *Crisis and Development: An Ecological Case Study of the Forest of Arden 1570–1674*, Cambridge University Press, 1978.

67* M. Spufford, *Contrasting Communities: English Villagers in the Sixteenth and Seventeenth Centuries*, 2nd edn, Cambridge University Press, 1979.

68   J. Thirsk, *English Peasant Farming: The Agrarian History of Lincolnshire from Tudor to Recent Times*, Routledge, 1957.

69   R. Tubbs, 'The development of smallholding and stock-keeping economy in the New Forest', *Agricultural History Review*, 13, 1965.

70   G. H. Tupling, *The Economic History of Rossendale*, Chetham Society, 1927.

71   D. Underdown, 'The chalk and the cheese: contrasts among English Clubmen', *P. & P.*, no. 85, 1979.

72   S. J. and S. J. Watts, *From Border to Middle Shire: Northumberland 1586–1625*, Leicester University Press, 1975.

73* K. Wrightson and D. Levine, *Poverty and Piety in an English Village: Terling 1525–1700*, 2nd edn, Academic Press, 1995.

74   K. Wrightson and D. Levine, *The Making of an Industrial Society: Whickham 1560–1765*, Clarendon Press, 1991.

FAMILY, KINSHIP AND OTHER SOCIAL RELATIONSHIPS:

75* M. Anderson, *Approaches to the History of the Western Family 1500–1914*, Macmillan, 1980.

76   M. Chaytor, 'Household and kinship: Ryton in the late sixteenth and early seventeenth centuries', *History Workshop*, 10, 1980.

77   D. Cressy, 'Kinship and kin interaction in early modern England', *P. & P.*, no. 13, 1986.

78   K. M. Davies, 'Continuity and change in literary advice on marriage', in R. B. Outhwaite (ed.), *Marriage and Society: Studies in the Social History of Marriage*, Europa Publications, 1981.

79   V. B. Elliott, 'Single women in the London marriage market: age, status and mobility 1598–1619', in ibid.

80   R. Adair, *Courtship, Illegitimacy and Marriage in Early Modern England*, Manchester University Press, 1996.

81   J. Goody, J. Thirsk and E. P. Thompson (eds), *Family and Inheritance: Rural Society in Western Europe 1200–1800*, Cambridge University Press, 1976.

82   P. E. H. Hair, 'Bridal pregnancy in rural England in earlier centuries', *Population Studies*, 20, 1966.

83   J. Hajnal, 'European marriage patterns in perspective', in D. V. Glass and D. E. C. Eversley (eds), *Population in History: Essays in Historical Sociology*, Arnold, 1965.

84   M. Ingram, *Church Courts, Sex and Marriage in England 1570–1640*, Cambridge University Press, 1987.

85   R. Houlbrooke, *Church Courts and People during the English Reformation*, Cambridge University Press, 1979.

86* R. Houlbrooke, *The English Family 1450–1700*, Longman, 1984.

87   P. Laslett, K. Oasterveen and R. M. Smith (eds), *Bastardy and its Comparative History*, Arnold, 1980.

88   P. Laslett, *Family Life and Illicit Love in Earlier Generations*, Cambridge University Press, 1977.

89 P. Laslett and R. Wall (eds), *Household and Family in Past Time*, Cambridge University Press, 1972.

90 D. Levine, *Family Formation in an Age of Nascent Capitalism*, Academic Press, 1977.

91 M. Macdonald, *Mystical Bedlam: Madness, Anxiety and Healing in Seventeenth-Century England*, Cambridge University Press, 1981.

92 A. Macfarlane, *The Family Life of Ralph Josselin*, Cambridge University Press, 1970.

93 L. Pollock, *Forgotten Children: Parent–Child Relations from 1500–1900*, Cambridge University Press, 1983.

94 G. J. Schochet, *Patriarchalism in Political Thought*, Basic, 1975.

95 M. Slater, *Family Life in the Seventeenth Century: The Verneys of Claydon House*, Routledge, 1984.

96 L. Stone, *The Family, Sex and Marriage in England 1500–1800*, Weidenfeld 1977; abridged paperback edn, Penguin 1979. See the critical reviews by K. Thomas, *Times Literary Supplement* (21 October 1977), E. P. Thompson, *New Society*, September 1977, and A. Macfarlane, *History and Theory*, xviii, 1979.

97 M. Todd, 'Humanists, puritans and the spiritualised household', *Church History*, 49, 1980.

98 K. Wrightson, 'Household and kinship in sixteenth-century England', *History Workshop*, 11, 1981.

WOMEN

99 S. Amussen, *An Ordered Society: Gender and Class in Early Modern England*, Oxford University Press, 1989.

100*B. Capp, 'Separate domains? Women and authority in early modern England', in P. Griffiths, A. Fox and S. Hindle (eds), *The Experience of Authority in Early Modern England*, Macmillan, 1996.

101 L. Charles and L. Duffin (eds), *Women and Work in Pre-Industrial England*, Croom Helm, 1985.

102 A Clark, *Working Life of Women in the Seventeenth Century*, Routledge, 1919.

103 P. Crawford, *Women and Religion in England 1500–1720*, Routledge, 1993.

104 P. Earle, 'The female labour market in London in the later seventeenth and early eighteenth centuries', *Econ. H. R.*, 42, 1989.

105 A. L. Erickson, *Women and Property in Early Modern England*, Routledge, 1993.

106 A. Fletcher, 'The male dilemma: the future of patriarchy in England 1560–1660', *T. R. H. S.*, 6th series, 4, 1994.

107 A. Fraser, *The Weaker Vessel: Woman's Lot in Seventeenth-Century England*, Weidenfeld, 1984.

108 P. Higgins, 'The reaction of women' in B. Manning (ed.), *Politics, Religion and the English Civil War*, Arnold, 1973.
109 C. Holmes, 'Women: witnesses and witches', *P.& P.*, no. 140, 1993.
110 J. I. Kermode and G. Walker (eds), *Women, Crime and the Courts in Early Modern England*, University College London Press, 1994.
111*A. Laurence, *Women in England 1500–1760: A Social History*, Weidenfeld, 1994.
112 M. Prior (ed.), *Women in English Society 1500–1800*, Routledge, 1985.
113 J. Sharpe, 'Witchcraft and women in seventeenth-century England: some northern evidence', *Change and Continuity*, 6, 1991.
114 K. Thomas, 'Women and the Civil War sects', *P. & P.*, no. 13, 1958.
115 R. Thompson, *Women in Stuart England and America: A Comparative Study*, Routledge, 1974.
116 D. Underdown, 'The taming of the scold and the enforcement of patriarchal authority in early modern England', in A. Fletcher and J. Stevenson (eds), *Order and Disorder in Early Modern England*, Cambridge University Press, 1985.

ADOLESCENTS:

117*I. K. Ben-Amos, *Adolescence and Youth in Early Modern England*, New Haven, 1994.
118 P. Griffiths, *Youth and Authority: Formative Experiences in England 1560–1640*, Oxford University Press, 1996.
119 P. Griffiths, 'Masterless young people in Norwich 1560–1645', in P. Griffiths, A. Fox and S. Hindle (eds), *The Experience of Authority in Early Modern England*, Macmillan, 1996.
120 S. R. Smith, 'The London apprentices as seventeenth-century adolescents', *P & P.*, no. 61, 1979.

LOCAL COMMUNITIES AND THE NATION:

121 B. Bushaway, *Custom, Ceremony and Community in England 1700–1880*, Junction Books, 1982.
122 P. Clark, *English Provincial Society from the Reformation to the Revolution: Politics and Society in Kent 1500–1640*, Harvester, 1977.
123 R. Cust and P. Lake, 'Sir Richard Grosvenor and the rhetoric of magistracy', *Bulletin of the Institute of Historical Research*, liv, 1981.
124 A. Everitt, *The Local Community and the Great Rebellion*, Historical Association pamphlet, 1969.
125 A. Everitt, 'The county community', in E. W. Ives (ed.), *The English Revolution 1600–60*, Arnold, 1968.
126 A. Everitt (ed.), *Suffolk and the Great Rebellion*, Suffolk Record Society, 1961.

127 A. Everitt, *The Community of Kent and the Great Rebellion*, Leicester University Press, 1966.
128 A. Fletcher, *A County Community in Peace and War: Sussex 1600–60*, Longman, 1975.
129*A. Fletcher, 'National and local awareness in the county communities', in H. Tomlinson (ed.), *Before the English Civil War*, Macmillan, 1983.
130 D. Hirst, *The Representative of the People? Voters and Voting in England under the Early Stuarts*, Cambridge University Press, 1975.
131 C. Holmes, 'The county community in Stuart historiography', *Journal of British Studies*, vii, 1980.
132 C. Holmes, *Seventeenth-Century Lincolnshire*, Lincolnshire Local History Society, 1980.
133 A. Hughes, *Politics, Society and Civil War in Warwickshire, 1620–60*, Cambridge University Press, 1987.
134 R. Hutton, *The Rise and Fall of Merry England: The Ritual Year 1400–1700*, Oxford University Press, 1994.
135 M. Ingram, 'Ridings, rough music and the "reform of popular culture" in early modern England', *P. & P.*, no. 105, 1984.
136 M. E. James, *Family, Lineage and Civil Society: A Study of Society, Politics and Mentality in the Durham Region 1500–1640*, Clarendon Press, 1974.
137 J. Morrill, *Cheshire 1630–60: County Government and Society during the 'English Revolution'*, Oxford University Press, 1974.
138 J. E. Neale, 'The Elizabethan Political Scene', *Proceedings of the British Academy*, 1948.
139 A. Hassell Smith, *County and Court: Government and Politics in Norfolk 1558–1603*, Clarendon Press, 1974.
140 D. Underdown, *Somerset in the Civil War and Interregnum*, David and Charles, 1973.
141 D. Underdown, *Revel, Riot and Rebellion: Popular Politics and Culture in England 1603–60*, Oxford University Press, 1985.

POPULATION:

142 A. B. Appleby, *Famine in Tudor and Stuart England*, Stanford University Press, 1978.
143 J. D. Chambers, *Population, Economy and Society in Pre-Industrial England*, Oxford University Press, 1972.
144 F. J. Fisher, 'Influenza and inflation in Tudor England', *Econ. H.R.*, 18, 1965.
145 C. Hill, 'Sex, marriage and the family in England', *Econ. H. R.*, 31, 1978.
146*R. A. Houston, *The Population History of Britain and Ireland 1500–1750*, Macmillan, 1992.
147 T. H. Hollingsworth, 'The demography of the British peerage', *Population Studies*, supplement, 18, 1964–5.

148   E. E. Rich, 'The population of Elizabethan England', *Econ. H. R.*, 2, 1949-50.
149   R. S. Schofield, 'The representativeness of family reconstitution', *Local Population Studies*, 8, 1972.
150   R. S. Schofield, 'The impact of scarcity and plenty on population change in England 1541-1871', *Journal of Interdisciplinary History*, 14, 1983.
151   P. Slack, 'The plague reconsidered. A new look at its origins and effects in sixteenth- and seventeenth-century England', *Local Population Studies*, supplement (1977).
152   P. Slack, *The Impact of Plague in Tudor and Stuart England*, Routledge, 1985.
153   R. M. Smith, 'Population and its geography in England 1500-1730', in R. A. Dodgson and R. A. Butlin (eds), *An Historical Geography of England and Wales*, Academic Press, 1978.
154   J. Thirsk, *Sources of Information on Population*, Phillimore, 1964.
155   E. A. Wrigley, 'Family limitation in pre-industrial England', *Econ. H. R.*, 19, 1966.
156   E. A. Wrigley, *An Introduction to Historical Demography*, Weidenfeld, 1969.
157   E. A. Wrigley and R. S. Schofield, *The Population History of England 1541-1871: A Reconstruction*, Arnold, 1981. See the reviews by M. W. Flinn in *Econ. H. R.*, 25, 1982, L. A. Clarkson in the *Times Higher Educational Supplement*, 5 February 1982, and D. Gaunt *et. al.* in *Social History*, 8, 1983.

PRICES AND WAGES:

158   A. B. Appleby, 'Grain prices and subsistence crises in England and France 1590-1740', *Journal of Economic History*, xxxiv, 1979.
159   P. Bowden, 'Agricultural prices, farm profits and rents', in 43.
160   P. Bowden, 'Agricultural prices, wages, farm profits and rent', in 44.
161   E. H. Phelps Brown and S. V. Hopkins, 'Seven centuries of the prices of consumables, compared with builders' wage rates', ibid., xxiii, 1956.
162   C. E. Challis, 'Spanish bullion and monetary inflation in England in the later sixteenth century', *Journal of European Economic History*, iv, 1975.
163   C. E. Challis, *The Tudor Coinage*, Manchester University Press, 1978.
164   C. E. Challis, 'The debasement of the coinage 1542-51', *Econ. H.R.* 20, 1967.
165   E. W. Gilboy, *Wages in Eighteenth-Century England*, Harvard University Press, 1934.
166   J. D. Gould, *The Great Debasement*, Clarendon Press, 1970.
167   H. A. Miskimin, 'Population growth and the Price Revolution in England', *Journal of European Economic History*, iv, 1975.

168*R. B. Outhwaite, *Inflation in Tudor and Stuart England*, 2nd edn, Macmillan, 1992.
169 J. E. Thorold Rogers, *A History of Agriculture and Prices in England*, 2 vols, Clarendon Press, 1866–1902.

STUDIES OF INDIVIDUALS, INDIVIDUAL FAMILIES AND SOCIAL GROUPS:

(a) Individuals and individual families

170 J. V. Beckett, *Coal and Tobacco: The Lowthers and the Economic Development of West Cumberland 1650–1760*, Cambridge University Press, 1981.
171 D. C. Coleman, *Sir John Banks: Baronet and Businessman*, Clarendon Press, 1975.
172 B. Coward, *The Stanleys, Lords Stanley and Earls of Derby 1385–1672*, Chetham Society, 1983.
173 C. Cross, *The Puritan Earl: The Life of Henry Hastings 3rd Earl of Huntingdon*, Macmillan, 1966.
174 P. Earle, *The World of Defoe*, Weidenfeld, 1976.
175 M. E. James, 'A Tudor Magnate and the Tudor State: Henry 5th Earl of Northumberland, *Borthwick Papers*, 30, York, 1966.
176 F. Manuel, *A Portrait of Isaac Newton*, Oxford University Press, 1968.

(b) The land-owning classes

177 G. R. Batho, 'Landlords in England', in 43.
178 J. V. Beckett, 'English landownership in the later seventeenth and eighteenth centuries: the debate and the problems', *Econ. H. R.*, 30, 1977.
179 B. G. Blackwood, *The Lancashire Gentry and the Great Rebellion*, Chetham Society, 1978.
180 L. Bonfield, *Marriage Settlements 1601–1740: The Adoption of the Strict Settlement*, Cambridge University Press, 1983.
181 J. Broad, 'Gentry finances and the Civil War – the case of the Buckinghamshire Verneys', *Econ. H. R.*, 32, 1979.
182 J. T. Cliffe, *The Yorkshire Gentry from the Reformation to the Civil War*, Athlone Press, 1969.
183 B. Coward, 'Disputed inheritances: some difficulties of the nobility in the later sixteenth and early seventeenth centuries', *Bulletin of the Institute of Historical Research*, 44, 1971.
184 M. Davies, 'Country gentry and payment to London 1650–1714', *Econ. H. R.*, 24, 1971.
185 H. J. Habakkuk, 'English landownership 1680–1740', *Econ. H. R.*, 1st series, 10, 1940.
186 H. J. Habakkuk, 'Landowners and the Civil War', *Econ. H.R.*, 18, 1965.

187 H. J. Habakkuk, 'Public finance and the sale of confiscated lands during the Interregnum', *Econ. H. R.*, 15, 1962.

188 H. J. Habakkuk, *Marriage, Debts and the Estate System: English Landownership 1650–1950*, Oxford University Press, 1994.

189*F. Heal and C. Holmes, *The Gentry of England and Wales 1500–1700*, Macmillan, 1994.

190 B. A. Holderness, 'The English land market in the eighteenth century: the case of Lincolnshire', *Econ. H.R.*, 27, 1974.

191 G. E. Mingay, *English Landed Society in the Eighteenth Century*, Batsford, 1963.

192 G. E. Mingay, *The Gentry*, Longman 1976.

193 L. Stone, *The Crisis of the Aristocracy 1558–1641*, Oxford University Press, 1965; abridged paperback edn, OUP, 1967. See the reviews by G. Aylmer in *P. & P.*, no. 32, 1965, D. Coleman in *History*, li, 1966, R. Ashton in *Econ. H. R.*, 22, 1969, A. Everitt in *Agricultural History Review*, 16, 1968, J. Hexter in *Journal of British Studies*, 8, 1968; and the comments by C. Russell & C. Thompson in *Econ. H. R.*, 25, 1972.

194 L. Stone. (ed.), *Social Change and Revolution in England*, Longman, 1965.

195 L. Stone and J. C. F. Stone, *An Open Elite? England 1540–1880*, Clarendon Press, 1984.

196 R. H. Tawney, 'The rise of the gentry 1558–1640', *Econ. H. R.*, 1st series, 11, 1941.

197 J. Thirsk, 'The sale of royalist lands during the Interregnum', *Econ. H.R.*, 5, 1952–3.

198 J. Thirsk, 'The Restoration land settlement', *Journal of Modern History*, 26, 1954.

(c) Yeomen and husbandmen.

199 J. V. Beckett, 'The decline of the small landowner in eighteenth and nineteenth-century England: some regional considerations', *Agricultural History Review*, xxx, 1982.

200*M. Campbell, *The English Yeoman*, Yale University Press, 1942.

201 A. H. Johnson, *The Disappearance of the Small Landowner*, Clarendon Press, 1909.

202 E. Kerridge, *Agrarian Problems in the Sixteenth Century and After*, Allen and Unwin, 1969.

203 G. E. Mingay, 'The size of farms in the eighteenth century', *Econ. H. R.*, 14, 1962.

204*R. H. Tawney, *The Agrarian Problem in the Sixteenth Century*, Longman, 1912.

205 J. R. Wordie, 'Social change on the Leveson-Gower estates', *Econ. H. R.*, 27, 1974.

(d)Labourers, servants and vagrants.

206 A. L. Beier, 'Vagrants and the social order in Elizabethan England', *P. & P.*, no. 64, 1974.

207 A. L. Beier, *Masterless Men: The Vagrancy Problem in Britain 1500–1640*, Methuen, 1985.

208 D. C. Coleman, 'Labour in the English economy of the seventeenth century', *Econ. H. R.*, viii, 1956.

209*A. Everitt, 'Farm labourers', in 43.

210 A. Kussmaul, *Servants in Husbandry in Early Modern England*, Cambridge University Press, 1981.

211 J. Rule, *The Experience of Labour in Eighteenth-Century Industry*, Croom Helm, 1981.

212 P. Slack, 'Vagrants and vagrancy in England 1598–1664', *Econ. H. R.*, 28, 1974.

213 K. Snell, *Annals of the Labouring Poor: Social Change and Agrarian England 1600–1900*, Cambridge University Press, 1985.

(e)Merchants, civil servants and professionals.

214 G. Aylmer, *The King's Servants: The Civil Service of Charles I*, Routledge, 1959.

215 R. Brenner, *Merchants and Revolution: Commercial Change, Political Conflict and London's Overseas Trades 1550–1653*, Cambridge University Press, 1993.

216 J. Brewer, *The Sinews of Power: War, Money and the English State 1688–1783*, Unwin Hyman, 1989.

217 C. Brooks, 'Professions, ideology and the middling sort in the late sixteenth and early seventeenth centuries' in 16.

218 F. W. Brooks, 'The social position of the parson in the sixteenth century', *British Archaeological Association Journal*, x, 1948.

219 P. G. M. Dickson, *The Financial Revolution in England*, Macmillan, 1967.

220 R. Grassby, *The Business Community of Seventeenth-Century England*, Cambridge University Press, 1996.

221 C. Hill, *Economic Problems of the Church from Archbishop Whitgift to the Long Parliament*, Clarendon Press, 1958.

222 C. Hill, 'The medical profession and its radical critics', in his *Change and Continuity in Seventeenth-Century England*, Weidenfeld, 1974.

223 G. Holmes, *British Politics in the Age of Anne*, Macmillan, 1967.

224 G. Holmes, *The Trial of Dr Sacheverell*, Eyre Methuen, 1973.

225*G. Holmes, *Augustan England: Professions, State and Society 1680–1730*, Allen and Unwin, 1982.

226 R. Lang, 'Social origins and social aspirations of Jacobean London merchants', *Econ. H. R.*, xxvii, 1974.

227 R. O'Day, *The English Clergy: The Emergence and Consolidation of a Profession*, Leicester University Press, 1979.

228 W. R. Prest, *The Inns of Court under Elizabeth I and the Early Stuarts*, Longman, 1972.

229 *W. R. Prest, (ed.), *The Professions in Early Modern England*, Croom Helm, 1989.

230 J. H. Pruett, *The Parish Clergy Under The Later Stuarts: The Leicestershire Experience*, Leicester University Press, 1978.

231 J. H. Raach, *A Directory of English Physicians*, Dawson Pall Mall, 1962.

232 H. Roseveare, *The Treasury 1660–1870*, Allen Lane, 1973.

POVERTY AND POOR RELIEF:

233 T. Arkell, 'The incidence of poverty in the late seventeenth century', *Social History*, 12, 1987.

234 A. L. Beier, D. Cannadine and J. H. Rosenheim, 'Poverty and progress in early modern England' in A. L. Beier *et. al.*, (eds), *The First Modern Society*, Cambridge University Press, 1989.

235 W. G. Bittle and R. Todd Lane, 'Inflation and philanthropy in England: a reassessment of Jordan's data', *Econ. H. R.*, xxix, 1976.

236 J. F. Hadwin, 'Deflating philanthropy', *Econ. H. R.*, xxxi, 1978.

237 W. K. Jordan, *Philanthropy in England 1486–1660*, Allen and Unwin, 1959.

238 J. Pound, *Poverty and Vagrancy in Tudor England*, 2nd edn, Longman, 1986.

239 P. Slack, *Poverty and Policy in Tudor and Stuart England*, Longman, 1988.

240 G. Taylor, *Problems of Poverty 1660–1834*, Longman, 1969.

241 J. Walter, 'The social economy of dearth in early modern England' in R. Schofield and J. Walter (eds), *Famine, Disease and the Social Order*, Cambridge University Press, 1989.

RIOTS AND DISTURBANCES:

242 A. Charlesworth (ed.), *An Atlas of Rural Protest in Britain 1548–1800*, Croom Helm, 1982.

243 P. Clark, 'Popular protest and disturbance in Kent 1558–1640', *Econ. H. R.*, 29, 1976.

244 E. Hobsbawm and G. Rude, *Captain Swing*, Lawrence and Wishart, 1969.

245 K. Lindley, *Fenland Riots and the English Revolution*, Heinemann, 1982.

246 R. Manning, *Village Revolts: Social Protest and Popular Disturbances in England and Wales 1509–1640*, Oxford University Press, 1988.

247 B. Sharp, *In Contempt of all Authority: Rural Artisans and Riot in the West of England 1586–1660*, University of California Press, 1980.

248*P. Slack (ed.), *Rebellion, Popular Protest and the Social Order in Early Modern England*, Cambridge University Press, 1989.
249 E. P. Thompson, 'The moral economy of the English crowd in the eighteenth century', *P. & P.*, no. 50, 1971.
250 J. Walter and J. Morrill, 'Order and disorder in the English Revolution', in A. Fletcher and J. Stevenson (eds), *Order and Disorder in Early Modern England*, Cambridge University Press, 1985.
251 J. Walter, 'The Oxfordshire Rising of 1596', *P. & P.*, no. 107, 1985.
252 J. Walter and K. Wrightson, 'Dearth and the social order in early modern England', *P. & P.*, no. 71, 1976.

CRIME:

253 J. Brewer and J. Styles (eds), *An Ungovernable People: The English and their Law in the Seventeenth and Eighteenth Centuries*, Hutchinson, 1980.
254 J. Sharpe, 'Domestic homicide in early modern England', *Historical Journal*, xxiv, 1981.
255*J. Sharpe, *Crime in Seventeenth-Century England: A County Study*, Cambridge University Press, 1983.
256 J. Sharpe, *Crime in Early Modern England 1556–1750*, Longman, 1984.
257 L. Stone, 'Interpersonal violence in English society 1300–1980', *P. & P.*, no. 101, 1983.

URBAN SOCIETY:

258 I. Archer, *The Pursuit of Stability: Social Relations in Elizabethan London*, Cambridge University Press, 1991.
259 A. L. Beier and R. Finlay (eds), *The Making of the Metropolis: London 1500–1700*, Longman, 1986.
260 P. Borsay, *The English Urban Renaissance*, Oxford University Press, 1989.
261*P. Borsay (ed.), *The Eighteenth-Century Town*, Longman, 1990.
262*J. Barry (ed.), *The Tudor and Stuart Town*, Longman, 1990.
263 J. L. Boulton, *Neighbourhood and Society: A London Suburb in the Seventeenth Century*, Cambridge University Press, 1987.
264 P. Clark, (ed)., *The Early Modern Town: A Reader*, Longman, 1976.
265 P. Clark and P. Slack (eds), *Crisis and Order in English Towns 1500–1700*, Routledge, 1972.
266 P. Corfield, *The Impact of English Towns, 1700–1800*, Oxford University Press, 1982.
267 P. Earle, *The Making of the English Middle Classes: London 1660–1732*, Methuen, 1989.
268 P. Earle, *A City Full of People: Men and Women in London 1650–1750*, Methuen, 1994.

269 J. Ellis, 'A dynamic society: social relations in Newcastle-uponTyne 1660–1760', in P. Clark (ed.), *The Transformation of English Provincial Towns 1600–1800*, Hutchinson, 1984.

270 F. J. Fisher, 'The development of London as a centre of conspicuous consumption in the sixteenth and seventeenth centuries', *T. R. H. S.*, 4th series, 30, 1948.

271 F. J. Fisher, 'London as an "engine of economic growth" ', in 258.

272 R. W. Herlan, 'Social articulation and the configuration of parochial poverty in London at the eve of the Restoration', *Guildhall Studies in London History*, 2, 1976.

273 V. Pearl, 'Change and stability in seventeenth-century London', *London Journal*, 5, 1979.

274 J. F. Pound, 'The social and trade structure of Norwich 1525–75', in 255.

275 M. Power, 'East and west in early modern London', in E. W. Ives, R. J. Knecht and J. J. Scarisbrick (eds), *Wealth and Power in Tudor England*, Athlone Press, 1978.

276 S. Rappaport, *Worlds Within Worlds: the Structure of Life in Sixteenth-Century London*, Cambridge University Press, 1989.

277 R. G. Wilson, *Gentlemen Merchants: The Merchant Community in Leeds 1700–1830*, Manchester University Press, 1971.

278 E. A. Wrigley, 'A simple model of London's importance ... 1650–1750', *P. & P.*, no. 37, 1967.

THE GROWTH OF A CONSUMER SOCIETY:

279 R. Berger, 'The development of retail trade in provincial England c.1550–1700', *Journal of Economic History*, 40, 1980.

280 J. Brewer and R. Porter (eds), *Consumption and the World of Goods*, Routledge, 1993.

281 D. E. C. Eversley, 'The home market and home demand 1750–1850', in E. L. Jones and G. E. Mingay (eds), *Land Labour and Population in the Industrial Revolution*, Arnold, 1967.

282 W. G. Hoskins, 'The rebuilding of rural England 1570–1640', *P. & P.*, no. 4, 1953.

283 R. Machin, 'The Great Rebuilding: a reassessment', *P. & P.*, no. 77, 1977.

284*N. McKendrick, 'The birth of a consumer society' and 'The consumer revolution of eighteenth-century England', in N. McKendrick, J. Brewer and J. H. Plumb (eds), *The Birth of a Consumer Society*, Hutchinson, 1982.

285 H. C. and L. H. Mui, *Shops and Shopkeeping in Eighteenth-century England*, Routledge, 1989.

286 J. H. Plumb, 'The commercialization of leisure in eighteenth-century England', in ibid.

287 M. Spufford, *The Great Reclothing of Rural England*, Hambledon Press, 1984.

288 J. Thirsk, *Economic Policy and Projects: The Development of a Consumer Society in Early Modern England*, Clarendon Press, 1978.

289 L. Weatherill, *Consumer Behaviour and Material Culture in Britain 1660–1700*, Routledge, 1988.

EDUCATION AND LITERACY:

290 P. Burke, *Popular Culture in Early Modern Europe*, Temple Smith, 1978.

291 B. Capp, *Astrology and the Popular Press: English Almanacs 1500–1800*, Faber, 1979.

292 K. Charlton, *Education in Renaissance England*, Routledge, 1965.

293 D. Cressy, *Literacy and the Social Order: Reading and Writing in Early Modern England*, Cambridge University Press, 1980.

294*D. Cressy (ed.), *Education in Tudor and Stuart England*, Arnold, 1975.

295 N. Hans, *New Trends in Education in the Eighteenth Century*, Routledge, 1951.

296 M. G. Jones, *The Charity School Movement of the Eighteenth Century*, Cambridge University Press, 1938.

297 T. Lacqueur, 'The cultural origins of popular literacy in England 1550–1850', *Oxford Review of Education*, 2, 1976.

298 V. E. Neuburg, *Popular Education in Eighteenth-Century England*, Woburn Press, 1971.

299 R. O'Day, *Education and Society 1500–1800: The Social Foundation of Education in Early Modern Britain*, Longman, 1982.

300 N. Orme, *English Schools in the Middle Ages*, Methuen, 1973.

301 J. Simon, *Education and Society in Tudor England*, Cambridge University Press, 1966.

302 C. J. Sommerville, *Popular Religion in Restoration England*, University Presses of Florida, 1977.

303 M. Spufford, 'First steps in literacy', *Social History*, 4, 1979.

304 M. Spufford, *Small Books and Pleasant Histories: Popular Fiction and its Readership in Seventeenth-Century England*, Cambridge University Press, 1985.

305 L. Stone, 'The educational revolution in England 1560–1640', *P. & P.*, no. 28, 1964.

306 L. Stone, 'Literacy and education in England 1640–1900', *P. & P.*, no. 42, 1969.

307 E. P. Thompson, 'Patrician society, plebeian culture', *Journal of Social History*, 7, 1974.

308 T. Watt, *Cheap Print and Popular Piety 1550–1640*, Cambridge University Press, 1993.

THE IMPACT OF PROTESTANTISM:

309 J. Bossy, *The English Catholic Community 1570–1850,* Darton, Longman and Todd, 1975.
310 J. Bossy, 'The character of English Catholicism', *P. & P.,* no. 21, 1962.
311 P. Collinson, *The Elizabethan Puritan Movement,* Cape, 1967.
312 P. Collinson, *The Religion of Protestants: The Church in English Society 1559–1625,* Oxford University Press, 1982.
313 P. Collinson, *English Puritanism,* Historical Association pamphlet, 1983.
314 P. Collinson (ed.), *Godly People,* Hambledon Press, 1984.
315*S. Doran and C. Durston, *Princes, Pastors and People: The Church and Religion in England 1529–1689,* Routledge, 1991.
316 E. Duffy, *The Stripping of the Altars: Traditional Religion in England 1400–1580,* Yale University Press, 1994.
317 A. Dures, *English Catholicism 1558–1642,* Longman, 1983.
318 A. Everitt, 'Nonconformity in country parishes', in J. Thirsk (ed.), *Land, Church and People,* British Agricultural History Society, 1970.
319 I. Green, *The Re-establishment of the Church of England 1660–1663,* Oxford University Press, 1978.
320 C. Haigh, *Reformation and Resistance in Tudor Lancashire,* Cambridge University Press, 1975.
321 C. Haigh, *English Reformations: Religion, Politics and Society under the Tudors,* Clarendon Press, 1993.
322 A. Macfarlane, *Witchcraft in Tudor and Stuart England,* Routledge, 1970.
323 P. McGrath, *Papists and Puritans under Elizabeth I,* Batsford, 1967.
324 J. Morrill, 'The Church', in his *Reactions to the English Civil War,* Macmillan, 1982.
325 J. J. Scarisbrick, *The Reformation and the English People,* Oxford University Press, 1984.
326 K. Thomas, *Religion and the Decline of Magic: Studies in Popular Beliefs in Sixteenth- and Seventeenth-Century England,* Weidenfeld, 1971.
327 N. Tyacke, *Anti-Calvinists: The Rise of English Arminianism 1590–1640,* Oxford University Press, 1990.
328 N. Tyacke, 'Popular puritan mentality in late Elizabethan England', in P. Clark, A. G. R. Smith and N. Tyacke (eds), *The English Commonwealth,* Leicester University Press, 1979.
329 M. Watts, *The Dissenters from the Reformation to the French Revolution,* Clarendon Press, 1978.

THE SCIENTIFIC REVOLUTION:

330 A. R. Hall, *The Revolution in Science 1500–1750,* Longman, 1983.
331*M. Hunter, *Science and Society in Restoration England,* Cambridge University Press, 1981.

332*A. G. R. Smith, *Science and Society in the Sixteenth and Seventeenth Centuries*, Thames and Hudson, 1972.

333 C. Webster, *The Great Instauration: Science, Medicine and Reform 1626–60*, Duckworth, 1975.

SOME PRIMARY SOURCES:

334 *The Autobiography of Richard Baxter*, ed. J. M. Lloyd Thomas, Dent, 1931.

335 *The Farming and Memorandum Books of Henry Best of Elmswell, 1642*, ed. D. M. Woodward, Oxford University Press for the British Academy, 1984.

336 *The Autobiography and Correspondence of Sir Simonds D'Ewes, Bart*, London, 1845.

337 J. H. Morehouse (ed.), 'The diurnall of Adam Eyre', in *Yorkshire Diaries*, Surtees Society, 75, 1875.

338 Richard Gough, *The History of Myddle*, ed. D. Hey, Penguin, 1981.

339 *The Description of England by William Harrison*, ed. G. Edelen, Cornell University Press, 1968.

340 *The Diary of Lady Margaret Hoby 1599–1605*, ed. D. Meads, Routledge, 1930.

341 *The Diary of Ralph Josselin*, ed. A. Macfarlane, Oxford University Press for the British Academy, 1976.

342 'A first draft of Gregory King's *Observations* from his notebook, 1695, and journal, 1696', in 347.

343 *Robert Loder's Farm Accounts 1610–20*, 3rd series, liii, Camden Society, 1936.

344 *The Diary of Roger Lowe of Ashton-in-Makerfield, Lancashire, 1663–74*, ed. W. L. Sachse, Longman 1938.

345 *The Life of Adam Martindale Written by Himself*, ed. R. Parkinson, Chetham Society, 1845.

346 *The Autobiography of Henry Newcome, MA*, ed. R. Parkinson, Chetham Society, 1852.

347 *The Diary of Samuel Pepys*, (eds), R. Latham and W. Matthew, 10 vols, G. Bell and sons, 1979–83.

348 *The Economic Writings of Sir William Petty*, ed. C. Hull, Cambridge University Press, 1982.

349 P. Slack (ed.), *Poverty in Early-Stuart Salisbury*, Wiltshire Record Society, 1975.

350 Sir Thomas Smith, *De Republica Anglorum*, ed. M. Dewar, Cambridge University Press, 1982.

351 *The Autobiography of William Stout of Lancaster 1665–1752*, ed. J. Marshall, Chetham Society, 1967.

352 R. H. Tawney and E. M. Power (eds), *Tudor Economic Documents*, 3 vols, Longman, 1924.

353 J. Thirsk and J. P. Cooper (eds), *Seventeenth-Century Economic Documents*, Oxford University Press, 1972.
354 *The State of England Anno Dom. 1600* by Thomas Wilson, ed. F. J. Fisher, Camden Miscellany, 16, Camden Society, 3rd series, 52, 1936.

INDEX